The Fairfax Cup. Venetian, late 15th century. A semi-opaque turquoise glass beaker painted in enamel colours and gilt. It is one of three glasses with enamel decoration on turquoise and is the only one with figures in which different episodes of a single classical legend are unfolded in sequence round the bowl. It tells the story of Pyramus and Thisbe from Ovid, *Metamorphoses*, Book IV (better known perhaps to English readers from *A Midsummer Night's Dream*) in three scenes. The one shown on this side is of Pyramus, followed by Thisbe, setting out for their trysting-place by the well—shown as a Renaissance fountain. The beaker belonged to the Fairfax family from before 1643. It was kept in a box in a wash-leather bag with traces of a seal and this note: 'In this bag is the Ancient Cup of our Familie putt into this bagg August 21st, 1694, by me, C. ffairfax.'

7

THE COUNTRY LIFE BOOK OF
GLASS

THE COUNTRY LIFE BOOK OF

GLASS

Frank Davis

LONDON: COUNTRY LIFE LIMITED

First published in 1966
by Country Life Limited
Tower House, Southampton Street, London, W.C.2
Printed in Great Britain by
Robert MacLehose & Company, Limited
The University Press, Glasgow

Contents

List of Plates

Acknowledgments

I wish to express my warm thanks to all those named below and to many others who have also been generous with their help:

British Museum: 1, 2, 23, 24, 34, 36

Victoria and Albert Museum: 3, 4, 5, 6, 7, 8, 9, 10, 11, 12, 13, 14, 15, 16, 17, 18, 19, 20, 21, 22, 25, 26, 27, 28, 29, 30, 31, 32, 33, 35, 40, 41, 42, 44, 45, 46, 47, 48, 49, 50, 51, 52, 53, 57, 58, 59, 60, 61, 62, 64, 65, 66, 68, 74, 81, 82, 83, 86, 87, 88, 98, 99, 101, 103, 104, 105, 106, 107, 108, 109, 110, 111, 115, 116, 117, 118, 119, 124, 125, 126, 127, 128, 129, Frontispiece

Christie's: 37, 39, 43

Sotheby's: 38, 54, 67, 69, 70, 71, 85, 89, 90, 91, 92, 93, 94, 95, 96, 97, 100

Philadelphia Museum of Art: 55

E. M. Elville: 56, 84, 113, 114

National Portrait Gallery: 63

Cecil Davis: 72, 73, 75, 76, 78, 79

Central Museum, Northampton: 77

F. Partridge and Sons: 80

Brod Gallery: 102

Mallett, Ltd.: 112

Orrefors Glassworks: 120, 121, 122, 123

Introduction

There is nothing original about this book beyond its manner of presentation. There are many volumes which deal with one or more aspects of the subject. Of these a certain number are out of print, others are high priced, a few are over-lavish of words. Many are highly technical and difficult to follow without a more than normal acquaintance with the techniques described; all of them, whether sold at half a guinea or at many guineas, are valuable for one reason or another. A selection from them is given in the bibliography.

This book merely attempts to sum up the result of generations of research in a convenient form and to provide the reader with just sufficient text and illustrations to form a launching pad for his own voyages of discovery, for things like these deserve to be studied closely and in three dimensions, and not merely in the pages of a book. The reader therefore is advised, if he is endowed with leisure, to spend what time he can in the British Museum, the Victoria and Albert Museum and elsewhere up and down the country wherever there are good public collections of glass (i.e. Oxford, Cambridge, Bedford and many more places), to haunt the auction rooms and to talk to the few dealers who specialise in this wholly fascinating material, which, at least since the discovery of glass-blowing, has made such an immense contribution to the amenities of civilisation. If he is able to go further afield he will inevitably visit also Murano and the Corning Museum in the United States.

1. Glass in Antiquity

If the Ancients had been more imaginative they would surely have added an Eighth Wonder of the World to their famous list of Seven. This Eighth Wonder is Glass, a metal which can reasonably be described as supremely beautiful though derived from humble materials, ductile, docile and submitting willingly to all kinds of manipulation. At various stages in its manufacture it can be moulded, twisted, painted, engraved, cut, or impregnated with colour: it can glow like a jewel or it can be as near shadowless and colourless as makes no matter; it can be purely decorative, or wholly useful, or both; and it has been as important to the march of science as it has been to the comfort and comeliness of the ordinary dining-table.

Pliny tells an impossible tale, often repeated, that the discovery of glass was accidental—that Phoenician sailors, after making a hearth on sand dunes from blocks of saltpetre they were carrying as cargo, lit a fire to cook with; as a result, translucent rivulets of some new fluid trickled forth. But glass is not made by fusing saltpetre and sand under intense heat; it is produced by the fusion in certain proportions of silica with an alkali. The silica came from quartz-sand with the addition of quartz pebbles and flints, the alkali from soda (obtained from burning seaweed) or from potash (derived from burning wood). Obviously soda-glass would be made in districts near the sea, potash-glass in wooded areas inland. The distinction is not without importance, because soda-glass becomes viscous at a lower temperature and remains for a longer time soft and malleable. Therefore it can be

1. One of the earliest glass vessels which can be dated. A jug in the British Museum. It bears the cartouche of Thothmes III of the 15th Dynasty (1501–1449 B.C.).

2. The Portland Vase.

3. Amphora-shaped vase from Tel
el-Amarna. 5th century B.C.

4. Amphora from the 5th century B.C.

5. Alabastron, late 5th century B.C.

6. Alabastron, late 4th or 3rd century
B.C.

7. Jug, 4th or 3rd century B.C.

8. Amphora, c.100 B.C., probably Alexandrian.

more easily moulded and manipulated. Potash-glass hardens more quickly; it is heavier and so lends itself more readily to cutting and engraving.

The Egyptians were covering their pottery wares with a thin film of glass by 2600 B.C. There is a fragment of a glass rod in Berlin which bears the cartouche of Amenemat III of the 12th Dynasty (2050–2000 B.C.), and in the Egyptian Museum in Cairo there are numerous beads and amulets of coloured glass intended as substitutes for precious and semi-precious stones, and these, it appears, go back to the 4th millenium B.C. The earliest glass *vessels* which can be dated are three vases with the cartouche of Thothmes III (15th Dynasty, 1501–1449 B.C.). One of these is in the British Museum (Fig. 1). The second, dark blue with yellow festoons, is in Munich, the third, of turquoise blue glass with a gold rim, in the Metropolitan Museum, New York. The early colour is a light green, the standard for many centuries. Next, by about 3000 B.C., blue of two kinds began to be used—a lapis lazuli blue and a turquoise with a greenish tinge. There is an amulet of blue glass bearing the cartouche of Antef IV (2420–2380 B.C.) of the 13th Dynasty in the British Museum; by the middle of the 2nd millenium B.C., the 'turquoise and sky-blues are of incomparable beauty' (I quote from Frederic Neuberg, who is not given to superlatives). Later colours became more varied—grey, yellow, black, brown and orange; later still they were red and green, the latter a true green, not merely a greenish tinge.

Methods of manufacture demanded a high degree of skill—methods which were described by Sir Flinders Petrie in the light of his excavations between 1891 and 1893 at Tel el-Amarna, Akhenaton's capital, built about 1375 B.C. Petrie's account is summarised by Neuberg as follows:

'A small linen bag was filled with sand and was tied by a thread to the narrow end of a tapering iron rod. A thread of glass was then wound round and round this bag until it was completely covered, and was then reheated and smoothed by marvering on a marble slab. While it was being worked, the piece was kept on the iron rod. After the glass had cooled off, the iron rod could easily

9. Roman glass plaque moulded with a design of Bacchanalian figures.

10. Mask in turquoise-green glass, 18th Dynasty.

11. Roman six-sided bluish-green jar, 1st or 2nd century A.D.

12. Bottle with hoops at top and bottom—a type frequently found in the West. The maker, Frontinus, had a glass-works in Northern France.

13. Jar and cover—used as an urn for the ashes of the dead, 1st century A.D. Found at Pozzuoli in Campania.

14. (*Above*) Small dolphin bottle, for oil for use in the bath and carried suspended from the waist.

15. (*Left*) Bowl of mosaic glass— perhaps one of the much admired Murrhine bowls described by Pliny.

be withdrawn on account of its tapering shape and its contraction on cooling and the bag of sand was then removed. Details (handle, base, rim and decoration) were added with the tongs after the piece had left the furnace but while it could still be manipulated. These vessels have stout walls, and the glass is opaque and coloured—most frequently copper-blue, less often malachite-green.

'If on cooling the surface was not smooth, it was ground and then polished, and where the orifice of the vessel permitted, as in the case of bowls and wide-mouthed amphoras, the inside surface was also treated in this way. By these means vessels of this type acquired an appearance which would lead anyone to think they were of azurite or malachite, and this deceptive appearance has been retained down to the present day in most specimens which have been preserved under favourable conditions.'

Obviously anything produced in this manner must have required a great deal of time as well as skill, and there could be no question of mass production. Nor was it possible to make anything of any size, so that only small flasks—the so-called balmsamaria and alabastra for perfumes—are found, and these must have been expensive. The threads of glass which provide the decoration were pressed into the material before the finishing process of grinding and polishing and were manipulated by means of a comb-like tool by which the craftsman could make a pattern of parallel lines or, by twisting, other simple designs.

As time passed, other devices became fashionable, first among them mosaic glass, which seems to have made its first appearance under the luxury-loving Ptolemies after the foundation of Alexandria in 331 B.C. Alexander's conquests and the foundation of the great city called after him were an immense stimulus to the Mediterranean world and, as one minor result, gave the glass industry of Egypt and of the Middle East new horizons. In this much-admired mosaic glass small pieces of glass of various colours were arranged in a pattern, or merely haphazardly, and allowed to fuse together in the furnace. Plaques of various shapes were used as jewellery or inlaid in furniture, and outer and inner surfaces were ground smooth; bowls could be made by reheating and pressing these plaques in a mould.

A popular variant of this mosaic glass was the pattern which began to be known during the Italian

Renaissance as *millefiori* or a thousand flowers—that is glass slabs, or bowls, the patterns on which resemble a bed of flowers. The most familiar objects of this sort in the modern world are glass paper-weights, mostly from the French factories of Clichy, St Louis and Baccarat, made during the middle of the 19th century, which, sold for a few francs or shillings apiece at the time they were manu-factured, now realise anything from £5 to £2,000 in the auction rooms: pretty novelties, few of whose makers knew that their ancestry could be traced so far back. A bundle of different coloured glass rods was heated and drawn out thin, and a cross-section made the pattern.

While Alexandria was the chief centre of the industry, there were numerous glass-workers through-out the Eastern Mediterranean, and to some unknown among them (tradition says at Sidon) must be credited the epoch-making discovery that glass could not only be moulded on a core, but blown in its semi-liquid state. This discovery, so simple that it has long been taken for granted, gave immense flexibility to the shapes possible with this magical material, and all subsequent developments derive from it. It happened about the time of the birth of Christ, and the results—after many decades of trial and error—were decisive. Glass-makers were at last freed from the traditions imposed by the techniques necessary for the making of ceramics and could embark upon voyages of discovery of their own. For one thing it was now possible to make glass nearly paper thin, and this led to a delicate type of glass-thread decoration round the exterior and, in due course, to such remarkable instances of superfine craftsmanship as the Portland Vase and the Auldjo Vase, both of which are in the British Museum.

The Portland Vase (Fig. 2), the most famous object of its kind in the world, was found in 1644 in a sarcophagus, probably that of the Roman Emperor Alexander Severus, who was killed in A.D. 235. It was preserved in the library of the Palazzo Barberini. Nearly a century and a half later Gavin Hamilton bought it for the Duchess of Portland, and, when her collection was sold in 1786, it was bought by the Duke for 7,000 guineas. Later it was deposited on loan to the British Museum. A lunatic smashed it into small fragments in 1845, but it was repaired, at first not too well, but later brilliantly, and finally became the property of the nation in 1945. Josiah Wedgwood made some remarkable copies of it in his jasper ware and several editions have been made by the firm since his day. No one succeeded in copying it in glass until 1876, when John Northwood senior produced an astonishingly accurate replica. The inner glass is a dark blue, the outer casing opaque white. The Auldjo Vase was found in 1834 in the Casa de Goethe in Pompeii, in two parts. One of them was presented to Madame Auldjo by the Prince of Capua, while the other passed on to the market. The two pieces were at last united and presented to the British Museum.

The method of manufacture required the most delicate skills. First, the vessel (usually, as in the Portland Vase, of a deep blue) while still hot was dipped into a crucible containing molten opaque

16. Two handled bowl. 1st century A.D. A type more common in silver.

17. Vase with collar of purple glass, probably Syrian. 3rd or 4th century A.D.

white glass. If both inner vessel and its casing cooled satisfactorily, the outer white layer was cut away in accordance with the intended design, the inner layer beneath providing a dark background. Foliage and figures were thus carved in relief from the opaque white outer casing, the underlying dark glass being either uncovered entirely or—and this is the point—showing through the white in various tones according to the depth of cutting. There are three vases executed in this technique in the Naples Museum, one of them an amphora, 30 cm. high and decorated with a design of amorini treading grapes, and in Florence there is a balsamarium with a Bacchic sacrificial scene. A much damaged glass not unlike the Portland Vase was found at Solberg in Norway. It was clearly highly prized, for it was mended in gold in the 5th or 4th century B.C.

It is curious—indeed inexplicable—that whereas Roman lapidaries were able to accomplish such remarkable feats of craftsmanship, no one seems to have thought of simple glass-cutting or glass-engraving until comparatively late in Imperial times. At first there were hoops and bands and trellis patterns, then vine leaves and inscriptions; finally three bottles exist from the end of the 4th century A.D. shallow-cut with representations of buildings on the coast at Puteoli (later Pozzuoli), the chief centre of the industry.

Seven characteristic examples of early Egyptian glass are illustrated here, all from the Victoria and Albert Museum (Figs. 3 to 9). Fig. 3 is a small amphora-shaped vase of fine quality, similar to one found in a grave at Thebes of the 18th Dynasty, with combed and zigzag decoration, and, owing to the dry climate, with no signs of surface decay or the iridescence which, to modern eyes, is so agreeable a feature of much of the ancient glass that has survived from more humid areas. The shapes in favour were, not unnaturally, those familiar to the glass-makers from vessels in carved hardstones from the distant past, and these shapes were in use for many centuries. Fig. 4 is one of many amphora-shaped vessels with small feet and two handles similar to those excavated on sites which can be dated to about 550–500 B.C. Of the alabastra of Figs. 5 and 6, the first is thought to belong to the second half of the 5th century B.C., the latter, with its fine feather-like markings, to the 4th or 3rd. The jug of Fig. 7, a sensible, elegant, well-pouring ancestor of all the good jugs produced in all kinds of materials during the past 2,500 years, belongs to the same period. The graceful amphora of Fig. 8 is probably Alexandrian of about 100 B.C.

To complete this selection from the vast amount of Egyptian glass which has survived for so many centuries there is (Fig. 10) a turquoise-green mask, a distinguished representative of a large class of miniature figures which were either pressed in moulds, or carved on the lapidary's wheel.

The conquest of Egypt by the Romans in 27 B.C. had far-reaching results for the glass industry which neither Mark Antony, nor Cleopatra, nor Augustus himself could possibly have foreseen. The invention of glass-blowing at about this time occurred just when the ancient world was controlled by a single and, by comparison with recent chaos, a remarkably efficient government. The new technique was able to spread over the whole extent of the Empire, so that, with a factory established at Rome itself in A.D. 14, the art travelled by way of the valley of the Rhone into Gaul, and by the 2nd century A.D. the glass-makers of the Rhineland had a reputation equal to those of Alexandria and Sidon; Cologne in particular was an important centre, and there is some evidence of the existence of glass-works in Britain. Moulding was, of course, still used for certain shapes—for instance, for the Bacchanalian figures of Fig. 9—and also moulding in combination with blowing. The freedom of trade consequent upon the *Pax Romana*, combined with the flexibility possible in blown glass, produced a great variety of notable shapes, both large and small, some as distinguished as the little group illustrated in Figs. 11 to 21.

Fig. 11, a six-sided jar, of bluish-green glass, belongs to the 1st or 2nd century A.D., and similar bottles with longer necks include many with moulded inscriptions on the base, apparently advertisements for medicines. Fig. 12 shows a greenish moulded cylindrical bottle with hoops at top and bottom. Such bottles were common in Western Europe. This one is signed by Frontinus, who

18. Syrian six-handled bowl. Handles and decoration on the body of blue glass.

flourished in the 3rd or 4th century at either Boulogne or Amiens. The fine jar and cover of Fig. 13 was found at Pozzuoli, the ancient Puteoli, in Campania, together with coins of the Emperor Titus (A.D. 79–81)—a cinerary urn. Coins, of course, are valuable evidence as far as they go, but it has to be borne in mind that they can be earlier than the vessel in which they are found. The engaging little so-called dolphin bottle—the name derived from the handles, which somewhat resemble dolphins— was filled with oil for use at the baths and was carried suspended from the waist. The one illustrated (Fig. 14), of a greenish colour, is similar to some found on the side of the Roman camp at Richborough in Kent.

A well-known example of mosaic glass (Fig. 15) dates probably from the 1st century A.D. and is from Alexandria. It may be one of the Murrhine bowls described by Pliny and mentioned by other classical writers, though it is not clear whether Pliny was speaking of bowls made of coloured semi-precious hardstones such as agate or sardonyx, or of the glass-maker's imitations. In any case, these rare mosaic pieces, which were articles of luxury from the moment they were made, stem from the age-old Egyptian tradition of a multi-coloured pattern in hardstones. The glass-makers, with their ductile material, fused sections of coloured fragments together to make a kaleidoscopic pattern with infinite gradations of colour when seen by transmitted light.

Both form and decoration, sometimes fanciful, are more often than not distinguished, as if these quite humble workmen had an instinctive feeling for the possibilities and limitations of their material. Cutting was used sparingly, except in the case of certain rare vessels, and few examples of pictorial engraving have survived. In addition to forms derived from familiar pottery shapes, there

19. Flask with trefoil mouth, 3rd century A.D.

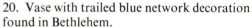

20. Vase with trailed blue network decoration found in Bethlehem.

21. Greenish jug with fantastic handles on the right, with two other vessels. Probably Syrian, 4th or 5th century A.D.

are some clearly borrowed from silver, of which Fig. 16 is a noteworthy example—a massive bowl with loop handles very like those of 1st-century silver cups apparently cut out of solid glass. The illustrations Figs. 17 to 21 must suffice to show the combination of playfulness and feeling for form which, on the whole, is so marked a characteristic of Roman glass, from whatever area, of the first four centuries of our era.

It is necessary to note that, apart from the normal elegance of form and decoration, Roman glass (like ancient Chinese bronzes) owes a great deal of its visual appeal to mere chance—that is, to the chemical changes produced by many centuries of burial in damp soil. The glass decays on the surface, light is broken up prismatically and the result is a most attractive iridescence. If the vessel is immersed in water the iridescence vanishes, but it reappears as soon as the piece is dried.

A few examples of enamel painting on Roman glass are recorded and also fragmentary pieces of so-called gold glasses, that is gold-leaf laid upon glass and engraved and then protected by a layer of glass over it. This is a technique which came to be known as *églomisé*, from the name of an 18th-century French picture-frame-maker named Glomy, who used this process in his business.

Finally, in this brief account of the glass in favour up to the first years of the Roman Empire in the West, mention must be made of the glasses known as *diatreta*—generally goblets or ceremonial drinking-vessels—which appear to have been fashioned from two separate layers. The inner one was left entirely smooth, but the outer was so undercut that it remained attached to the inner only at certain points, and the whole vessel seemed to have been made of two parts, one inside the other. The best known of these excessively rare objects is a small pail (*situla*) in the treasury of St Mark's at Venice.

2. Islamic Glass

The Mohammedan era dates from A.D. 622, the year of the Prophet's flight from Mecca to Medina. If any official in Rome or Constantinople heard of the flight, which is in the highest degree unlikely, he could scarcely be blamed if he failed to recognise its significance. It was one of those trivial happenings which excited barbarians, but was of no consequence to civilised mankind. The West was already in the hands of people who had swept down from the northern forests, but the great city which Constantine had founded on the Bosphorus seemed immutable. Who could imagine that in due course all the Near and Middle East, Egypt, North Africa and even Spain would fall an easy prey to a few wild desert fanatics, and that Constantinople itself would be swallowed up?

The traditions and a great deal of the skills of the Roman World lived on, subtly changing as the centuries passed; know-how was handed on by refugees from one threatened corner to another. Crusaders came and for a time occupied the fringe of the Levant—Tyre, Sidon, Aleppo, and other centres famous for glass-making; by the end of the 13th century they had gone, leaving nothing but their formidable castles and a reputation for greed. Some, returning home, brought with them as souvenirs some notable glass vessels, a few of which, considered sufficiently remarkable to be used as reliquaries, have been preserved in cathedral treasuries; fewer still are or have been in the possession of private families. Of the latter the best known is no doubt the cup known as the Luck of Eden Hall owned by the Musgrave family (Fig. 22). There is a tall cup in the Hope Collection in the British Museum painted with the Virgin and Child, St Peter and St Paul and angels, and a Latin dedication and prayer certainly Syrian. This was presumably a definite commission (Fig. 23).

 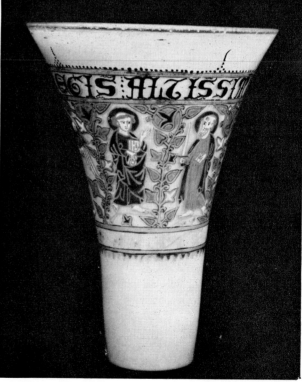

22. The Luck of Eden Hall. Syrian.   23. Tall cup painted with the Virgin and Child. SS Peter and Paul and angels. Hope Collection. Syrian.

24. The Aldrevandini beaker, painted with Swabian shields of arms. Syrian—perhaps Antioch.

Another famous Islamic vessel in the British Museum is the Aldrevandini beaker (Fig. 24), with Swabian shields of arms and the inscription 'Magister Aldrevandin[i] me Feci[t]'. It used to be thought that both these famous pieces were Venetian, but it now appears to be agreed that they belong to a period long before the glass industry was established in Venice. It is thought that Aldrevandini was probably an Italian employed in some Syrian workshop, possibly, suggests W. B. Honey, at a Frankish court such as that of the Princes of Antioch.

Islamic glass, except in very special cases, can no more be dated with any great precision than can the glass made during the hey-day of the Roman Empire, and its country of origin is frequently the subject of speculation. The Caliphs of Baghdad, for instance, attracted goods from as far away as China and workers from every corner of their vast domains—from Persia and Egypt, for example. Their Court moved to Samarra and remained there from 836 to 883, and excavations there just before the first World War afforded much evidence about both pottery and glass. The latter included mosaic glass, used for wall decoration, many small bottles for perfumes, and some cut-glass of great refinement with highly stylised designs of animals and foliage—most of it in fragments. Similar things have been found in widely different places, but, because of the evidence provided by the Samarra excavations, are definitely ascribed to the 9th century.

The art of glass-cutting was practised, though not, it would appear, very extensively, in Roman times, but just how and when is unknown. It is generally supposed to have been derived from carving on rock crystal, a mineral held in great respect and providing an obvious model for the glass-cutter. Various theories have been put forward: that it was a speciality of the Persians, or of the inhabitants of Basra, or of the Egyptians, the inheritors of several centuries of experience in this form of decoration. One of the finest rock crystal carvings in existence, a ewer in the treasury of St Mark's, Venice, is presumably Egyptian, for it bears a dedication to a Fatimid Caliph of Egypt who ruled from 975 to 996. A famous glass at Breslau, said to have belonged to St Hedwig, who died in 1243, is cut with a version of that common motif in Eastern Art, the Tree of Life, and there are similarly cut glasses in cathedral treasuries elsewhere; some of them have 13th-century metal mounts, and the general opinion now is that this whole group is Egyptian of the 11th or 12th century. Yet other

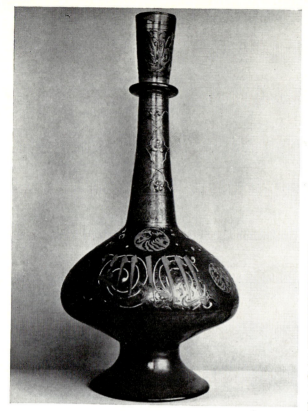

25. (*Above*) Possibly a Byzantine bottle, 7th or 8th century A.D.   26. (*Left*) Syrian enamelled glass, late 13th or early 14th century. Decorated with Chinese phoenixes, lotus and vine ornament.

pieces of cut-glass (in the treasury of St Mark's and in the Cathedral of Halberstadt in Saxony) have been ascribed to Persia, and also to Byzantium (Constantinople).

Experts have been very chary of attributing any surviving glass to the capital of the Eastern Empire, though it is not easy to believe that a city which dominated the known world for a thousand years until its capture by the Turks in 1453 did not contain one glasshouse of consequence within its walls. So far only one example of Byzantine glass has been identified with anything approaching certainty. This is a $4\frac{1}{2}$ in. wide bowl of purple glass decorated in enamels with rosettes, scroll-work, pseudo-Arabic script and figures in medallions resembling those on an ivory box in the Victoria and Albert Museum—the Veroli Casket, which, judging from its style, is perhaps of the 9th century. The enamelling corresponds with that described by Theophilus, a Westphalian monk who, at the end of the 10th century, compiled a *Schedula Diversarum Artium*, in which he included a section on glass; he refers to enamelled purple and sapphire-blue cups.

If the evidence of a Byzantine origin for this single cup is not wholly convincing, there seems to be none whatever for the other examples of early mediaeval glass which are its companions in the treasury of St Mark's. They are variously attributed to Syrian, Egyptian, Mesopotamian and Persian workshops. The majority are war-loot brought back from the sack of Constantinople in 1204 by the Venetians, who took part in the fourth Crusade.

There is, however, one early reference from which it is possible, not to prove, but to deduce a Byzantine origin for some of the shallow bowls at St Mark's. This is a description of the Church of St Sophia, written by Paul the Silentiary, for the opening ceremony in 563, in which single lights are described as balance-pans of silver in the centre of which rested cups of burning oil. It has been suggested that the bowls are the glass counterparts of these silver vessels. It has also been suggested that Byzantine glass is yellowish-toned, as distinct from the colourless metal of that which is probably Persian.

27. Small Syrian lamp enamelled with horsemen and falcons, *c*.1270.

The Victoria and Albert Museum very cautiously attributes the elegant bottle of Fig. 25 to Byzantium or Egypt of the 7th or 8th century.

In 1258 Baghdad was sacked by the Mongols under Hulagu and in 1260 Damascus escaped destruction only by unconditional surrender. In 1280 the Mongols overran China and founded the Yüan Dynasty. A side result of these world-shaking events was a certain amount of Chinese influence in design—vine ornament, cloud-scrolls, lotuses and peonies, for example—and a certain amount of trade. Syrian glasses were exported to China and celadon porcelain was sold in the Near East. The latter—a noble material in any case—was doubtless rendered more saleable by the suggestion that it was an infallible detector of poison. Fig. 26 shows a notable example of this Chinese influence— a bottle of about 1400 decorated with Chinese phoenixes, lotus and vine ornament. An earlier specimen from this area—perhaps about 1270 and thought to be from Damascus—is the elegant little lamp of Fig. 27, enamelled with figures of horsemen with falcons. Evidently Damascus was famous as a glass centre, for mediaeval inventories sometimes record glasses as '*de l'ouvrage de Damas*'.

As a result of excavations at Rakka in north-west Iraq certain vessels of clear metal decorated in white, gold or turquoise enamels are cautiously assigned to that place. The best known of these are two beakers preserved in the museums of Douai and Chartres, each of them with 13th- or 14th-century European silver gilt feet and mounts. The Douai beaker was part of a bequest recorded in 1329. Its leather case is with it and, from the arms on it, it seems likely that it was brought back from Palestine in 1251 by a crusader. Legend frequently gathers round such things (e.g. the Luck of Eden Hall), and the Chartres piece was said to have been a gift from Harun Al-Raschid to the Emperor Charlemagne.

Mediaeval man was no less credulous than the less sophisticated of his descendants and was fascinated not only by miracle-mongers and astrologers, but by the dream of turning base metals into gold. The equivalent of this alchemist's dream in the realm of glass-making was of course the artificial manufacture of precious and semi-precious stones. Coloured glass was frequently accepted as a precious stone of one sort or another and held in high honour. A few recorded instances must suffice.

A Roman blue glass cup in the cathedral treasury of Monza, said to have belonged to the Lombard Queen Theodolinda, who died in 628, was believed to have been cut from a sapphire. A slab of sapphire, mounted as an altar-table, was recorded in 1126 at Glastonbury, and at the Abbey of Reichenau on Lake Constance there is a green glass slab known as Charlemagne's emerald, reputed to have been given to him by the Byzantine Empress Irene, who died in 803. But by far the most famous of such glass objects is the *Sacro Catino* in the Cathedral of S. Lorenzo at Genoa—an emerald-green bowl taken by a Genoese crusader in the sack of Caesarea in 1101 and regarded as an emerald. It has been variously described as the Holy Grail, a gift from Solomon to the Queen of Sheba and the dish on which the head of St John the Baptist was carried by Salome. Another 'emerald' was a glass table, known as King Solomon's table, captured at Toledo in 711, and a third belonged to Tamerlaine at Samarkand in the early 15th century, while in 1472 the Shah of Persia honoured the Venetian *Signoria* with a bowl which is said to be of turquoise, but which is in fact turquoise-coloured glass. This, as well as the other glass vessels brought from Constantinople in 1204, is in the treasury of St Mark's.

But of all the many types of Islamic glass preserved in the great museums of the world, pride of place must be given to the lamps from Egyptian mosques—sumptuously enamelled and nobly proportioned. Though in ordinary speech they are usually referred to as lamps, they are in fact lanterns in which an oil vessel was placed. They were suspended from the roof by chains and were given a symbolic significance by a passage in the Koran, thus: 'God is the light of the Heavens and the Earth, His light is a niche in which is a lamp, the lamp in a glass, the glass as it were a glittering star.'

28. Syrian enamelled mosque lamp. It bears the name of the Mameluke Sultan of Egypt, Baybars II (1309–10).

29. Lamp from the Mosque
College of Sultan Hasan (died
1361) in Cairo. Decorated with lotus
and other flowers.

The majority of these lamps are inscribed with the names and titles of Mameluke sultans of Egypt or their officers of State—the Secretary, for instance, or the Master of the Wardrobe—frequently with their heraldic blazons, and consequently have an interest apart from the purely aesthetic or technical; for this was a violent, luxurious society in which a palace intrigue could promote a slave to wealth and influence at one moment and bring him to ruin or death at the next. All the lamps were made for Egyptian mosques, but not, it appears, in Egypt itself, but in Syria—at least until 1400, when Tamerlaine sacked Damascus and carried off most of the craftsmen to Samarkand.

Two magnificent examples of enamelled mosque lamps are illustrated in Figs. 28 and 29. Fig. 28 bears the name of the Sultan Baybars II (known as al-Jāshnigīr—the Taster), who deposed his master, the Sultan an-Nāsir Muhammad, and was the ruler of Egypt for a few months before his execution in 1310. The border of vine-ornament on the lower part is painted in red. The inscription—in itself the most graceful of ornaments—is translated as follows: 'Glory to our Lord the Sultan al-Malik al-Muzaffar, the Wise and Just, Pillar of the World and the Faith. May his victory be great.' The lamp of Fig. 29 comes from the Mosque College of Sultan Hasan, who died in 1361, and is unusual in that it is decorated with a design of lotus and other flowers clearly owing much to Chinese porcelain importations.

But the shape of things to come was unknowingly recorded by a man of Milan who visited Jerusalem in 1480. He said that glass vases from Murano were sent to Damascus for an official of the court of the Sultan Qāytbāy (1468–96). For the next two centuries Venice was destined to be the chief glass-making centre of the world.

3. Venice

There is no doubt that there were glass furnaces at Venice by the 11th century. The unique, the unbelievable city as we know it today, was then only beginning to rise from the waters and was not yet Mistress of the Adriatic; by the 13th century, she was well on the road to fortune, and, because of the danger of fires, banished the glass-makers to the island of Murano, which has been the centre of the industry ever since. There is no glass in existence which can be certainly identified as Venetian before the 15th century, but early paintings provide evidence of a modest range of goblets, flasks and decanter-shaped bottles. It is not known to what degree, if at all, the Venetian glass-workers derived their knowledge from Alexandria and other centres in the Eastern Mediterranean. Some authorities consider that there must have been numerous fairly close contacts, others—the majority —that the Near East had very little influence, but rather that the Venetians were carrying on a tradition which went back to their Roman predecessors.

It is curious, by the way, that, while there is ample documentation for Venice, there is next to none for Altare, near Genoa, where a glass-works was started by craftsmen from Normandy, whose productions were, for a time, serious rivals to those of the Venetians. But though contemporary records refer to both a *façon d'Altare* and a *façon de Venise*, no one, it appears, has succeeded in distinguishing between the two.

In Murano the industry was subject to strict regulation, aimed at preserving the secrets of the trade. The severe penalties against emigration frustrated the more adventurous spirits, but many good

30. Venetian ewer imitating chalcedony, *c*. 1600. 31. Venetian long-necked bottle imitating chalcedony, *c*. 1600.

32. Venetian bowl imitating chalcedony, *c*. 1600.

33. Late 15th-century Venetian goblet and cover. Derived from a prototype in silver.

34. Venetian nuptial goblet, *c*. 1480, with portraits of bride and bridegroom.

35. Venetian painted armorial dish, *c*. 1600.

36. Venetian nuptial goblet, *c*. 1480, with *Procession of Venus*.

37. *Façon de Venise* goblet. From the Netherlands, 17th century.

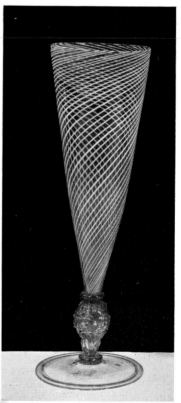

38. Venetian bowl—*latticino*.

39. Venetian tazza, diamond-engraved
with a coat of arms and foliage.

40. Venetian opaque white glass plate decorated with a view after Canaletto, 18th century.

craftsmen evaded the control and escaped, some to Altare, others to other Italian cities, or to the north. While it was difficult for the Muranese to leave home, the glass-makers of Altare were bound by no protectionist legislation and moved abroad freely. They went especially to nearby France, and also, with Venetian workmen, to Flanders, where the industry was established during the 16th century. Altare seems to have been remarkably enlightened and actually to have encouraged its people to teach others. It went so far that in 1495 its policy, directed by a highly organised corporation, the Universita dell' Arte Vitrea, was codified in a statute that seems to have been made expressly to encourage contacts abroad.

The result of all this was the emergence of an international style—or at least a style with a recognisable international accent—which came to be known as the *façon de Venise*—in the main based upon the know-how of the workshops of Murano. 'The diffusion of forms', writes Giovanni Mariacher, 'learned and imitated from those of Murano, reached such proportions at one time that it is occasionally difficult to distinguish the objects which originated from the glasshouses of the Lagoon from the copies made beyond the Alps. The difficulty is intensified by the fact that, at least in the early stages, these articles were often the handiwork of expatriate Murano craftsmen. A great many names, some of them belonging to the most famous glass-making families of Murano, are recorded in documents or other written sources as having worked in the various countries, thus fostering the development of an industry which was destined one day to offer formidable competition to that of Venice.'

In brief, national styles did in fact come about, but hardly until late in the 17th century. Meanwhile France, Germany, Spain and the Netherlands remained in debt to Altarists and runaways from Venice.

41. Venetian opaque white glass painted with flowers and a parrot, 18th century.

42. Venetian opaque white glass painted with a rural scene, 18th century.

43. South Staffordshire opaque white glass painted with a Chinese subject.　44. Spanish glass, 17th century.

The material used in the Venetian glasshouses was silica from quartz pebbles from the bed of the River Ticino and alkali from the ash of sea and marsh plants. The finished glass was dearer than its competitors, but had a smoky or pale yellow tone, and this fine *cristallo* or crystal glass, as it was called, was the envy of the rest of Europe from the 16th century onwards. Nor was the coloured glass less admired, and there are numerous vessels imitating semi-precious stones, such as onyx, agate and chalcedony. The three pieces of Figs. 30, 31 and 32 are characteristic examples of the glass-maker's skill in handling colours allied to a notable severity of form which was not greatly to the taste of later generations. They all three date from the late 16th or early 17th centuries and are clearly ancestors of the *Art Nouveau* fashions of three hundred years later. But not much can with any confidence be ascribed to the 15th century; an exception is no doubt the noble enamelled goblet and cover in the shape of a pyx (Fig. 33), obviously derived from a silver prototype and one of the finest objects in the Victoria and Albert Museum collection. It is sparingly decorated in gilt and with a small pattern in coloured enamels. Two others from the British Museum are also illustrated, each of them a nuptial goblet. One (Fig. 34) is painted with medallion portraits of a bride and bride-groom: the other (Fig. 36) is decorated with a carefree procession, very appositely, of Venus. The date of each is about 1480. The fine dish of Fig. 35 is inserted here to show the quality of early 16th-century armorial glass. Fig. 39 illustrates an armorial piece of about 1600: it is diamond-engraved. Another 15th-century glass, which was sold at Sotheby's in 1959 and is now in the Victoria and

45. Spanish glass—characteristic Andalusian proportions with winged handles.

46. (*Left*) Spanish glass water dropper. Catalonia, 17th or 18th century.

47. (*Below*) Two-handled vase from Andalusia.

Albert Museum, is the beaker known as the Fairfax Cup—an opaque turquoise-blue, enamelled with the story of Pyramus and Thisbe (Frontispiece).

But Venetian glass *par excellence*, from the 16th century onwards, does not depend upon forms borrowed from metal work, but stems directly from the skill and exuberant imagination of the glass-blower, at first in comparatively simple vessels and then, by the 17th century, in a myriad fanciful devices—all kinds of elongations and wavings and remarkably varied manipulations of the stems, culminating in such entertaining displays of virtuosity as vessels shaped as fishes, or flowers, or ships. This was a fashion which delighted the age irrespective of geography, and, as by now Italian craftsmen had established themselves in northern Europe, it is by no means always an easy matter to decide whether any given glass is a Murano export or a *façon de Venise* vessel made in Silesia, or Liége, or elsewhere to the north.

Among several methods devised for decorating clear glass was that known as *latticino*, a term applied to the manipulation of straight or spirally arranged threads of opaque glass embedded in the clear glass; the more intricate patterns produced by this means are known as lace-glass (*vetro de trina*). The method seems to have been in use by the middle of the 16th century and to have remained in fashion for more than two hundred years: a Venetian, Guiseppe Briati, who died in 1772, made a

48 and 49. *Façon de Venise*. Netherlands, 17th century.

50. *Façon de Venise* possibly French, 17th century. 51. *Façon de Venise*. Netherlands, possibly English, 17th century.

speciality of it. Consequently dating is more than ordinarily difficult. The splendid dish in the Buckley Gift at the Victoria and Albert Museum is generally regarded as dating from the 16th century. A tazza seen at Sotheby's in the summer of 1965 (Fig. 39) may be 17th-century or even 18th-century, and from Christie's is a 17th-century *façon de Venise* goblet (Fig. 37) from the Netherlands. Whatever their date, these *latticino* designs can be exceptionally attractive.

At this point, after mention of the use of opaque white glass threads in these *latticino* designs, it seems appropriate to refer to another manner in which opaque glass was put into service—that is, covering the whole surface, so that the vessel resembled porcelain. Very good 16th-century pieces are recorded, but the technique was not much in favour until the 18th century, owing, of course, to the popularity first of Chinese and then of European porcelain. White opaque glass, or, as it is more generally known, milk glass, can be enamel-painted like porcelain and, though more fragile and lighter, it looks not unlike it at a little distance. As one would expect, the Venetian glass manufacturers were not slow in producing ingenious souvenirs for tourists, views after Canaletto painted in red monochrome against a white background, for instance, such as Horace Walpole brought back to England in 1741. Figs. 40–42 are characteristic and fine examples of Venetian work of this

52. French
Pilgrim bottle of
marbled glass.

type, and similar glass was produced in England and northern Europe. A graceful English vase painted with flowering plants issuing from rocks and numerous Chinese figures (seen in the autumn of 1965 at Christie's) is a good example of South Staffordshire work of the period (Fig. 43).

Workmen from Murano were active at Antwerp in 1541, and one of them is recorded as having ventured as far east as Shiraz in Persia. From 1569 Venetian-style glass was made at Liége. Other glasshouses were at Middelburg and Amsterdam, at Cassel, Hall, in the Tyrol, and Nuremberg and at many places in Spain, Portugal, France and Germany. England honours Jacopo Verzelini as the father of the English glass industry. He obtained a privilege from Queen Elizabeth I in 1575 for twenty-one years to make Venice glasses in London and to teach Englishmen the craft. Figs. 44 to 52 show notable examples of late 16th- and 17th-century glasses which all owe a great deal to Venice fashions, but which, frequently, have a very definite national flavour. This is especially marked in the case of the Spanish designs of Figs. 44 to 47 and in that of glasses from the Netherlands and France (Figs. 48–52).

4. England and Ireland

Although Jacopo Verzelini is justly regarded as the patron saint of English glass-makers, he had predecessors who left marks, though small, and mostly indecipherable ones, on the pages of history. There is, for instance, a certain Laurence Vitrearius, i.e., the glass-maker (presumably of window-glass), who came from Normandy, settled half-way between Guildford and Petworth and was making glass for Westminster Abbey by about 1240. Others followed in the Weald country, annoying the local ironmasters by muscling in upon the diminishing supplies of wood. Fragments of both window and domestic glass have been excavated on the sites of glasshouses in the neighbourhood of Chiddingfold and Stane Street, but they reveal very little.

A fresh chapter began to be written—a preface to the Verzelini story—in 1549 when Protestant glass-makers from Lorraine came to England, headed by Jean Carré, of Arras and Antwerp, who obtained a licence in 1567 and set up a glasshouse at Alfold in Surrey. But hostility on the part of the local ironmasters dispersed Carré's men, who in 1570 broke with tradition and established a glass-house at Crutched Friars in London with the help of Italians, one of whom is believed to have been Jacopo Verzelini. Among Carré's Lorrainers were members of the Hennezel, Thisac, Thietry and Houx families, whose anglicised names—Henzey and Ensell, Tysack, Tittery, Hoe and How—are to

53. English diamond-engraved goblet by Verzelini, 1581.   54. English diamond-engraved Verzelini goblet, 1583. Motto of the Pewterers' Company engraved by Anthony de Lysle.

55. The Royal Oak goblet, possibly English. Portraits of Charles II and Catherine of Braganza.
Obverse and reverse.

be found among prominent glass-makers as far afield as Stourbridge and Newcastle-upon-Tyne. But Carré died in 1572 before his plans could achieve fruition.

It was Verzelini who built upon the foundations thus laid. The Crutched Friars glasshouse was burnt down in 1575; arson was and is still suspected, but proof is non-existent. The new Broad Street establishment was a success, thanks partly to demand by the best people, but chiefly to Verzelini's technical and commercial ability. After early opposition the glass-sellers who had previously imported their wares from Venice found it paid them just as well to distribute home-made goods. Harrison, in his *Description of England* of 1586, has this to say about the vogue for glass: 'It is a world to see in these our daies, wherein gold and silver most aboundeth, how that our gentilitie as lothing those metals (because of the plentie) do now generally choose rather the Venice glasses, both for our wine and beere . . . such is the nature of man generallie, that it most coveteth things difficult to be atteined. . . . And as this is seen in the gentilitie, so in the wealthie communaltie the like desire for glasse is not neglected. . . . The poorest also will have glasse if they may; but sith the Venetian is somewhat too deere for them, they content themselves with such as are made at home of ferne and burned stone.' This is an interesting sidelight upon the results of the newly discovered South American silver-mines and of Elizabethan pirate raids upon Spanish treasure-ships.

Fig. 53 is one of the Verzelini glasses in the Buckley Collection in the Victoria and Albert Museum, diamond-engraved with the names of John and Jone Dier. Fig. 54 is another goblet which appeared

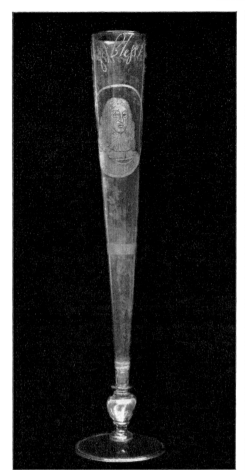 

56. The Exeter Flute, possibly English. Probably made for Charles II's Coronation. 57. English jug, boldly ribbed with rope-like handle, by Ravenscroft.

in a Sotheby sale during the 1962–63 season. It is dated 1583, engraved in diamond-point by Anthony de Lysle. The motto is that of the Pewterers' Company of London, for whom de Lysle is known to have worked—'In God is al mi trust'. (It was sold for £6,500.) So far the very few glasses definitely assigned to Verzelini's workshop have been of this character; others, undecorated and perhaps indistinguishable from Venetian work of his generation, are presumably in existence, though, in the case of such fragile material, glasses with an inscription are more likely to survive ordinary household hazards. Verzelini retired in 1592, three years before the expiry of his licence. He moved to Downe, in Kent, highly respected and with an adequate fortune. He died there in 1606, aged 84, and was buried in the parish church, commemorated by a brass tablet to the memory of himself, his wife and his children.

For nearly a century the record remains, not exactly blank, but obscure, for the industry—thanks to the system of monopolies—fell into the hands of commercial manipulators, very able men, but more interested in balance-sheets than in glass manufacture, tycoons of drive, imagination and *savoir-faire* and the type of *entrepreneur* who is a valuable asset to any industry, but does not necessarily take a pride in the quality of the product. On the retirement of Verzelini Sir Jerome Bowes took over the glasshouse and its workpeople and obtained a licence for twelve years, plus the sole right to import Venetian glass if he wished. By 1620 the trade was in the hands of the remarkable Sir Robert Mansell, who brought coal to London first from Fifeshire and then from Tyneside, when Scottish shipmasters raised the price to a point which he and the equally formidable Lady

58. The Butler Buggin bowl, 1676, by Ravenscroft.

59. English decanter jug with narrow neck, almost certainly by Ravenscroft.

60. English covered goblet, late 17th century.

61. Kit-Cat glass.   62. English sweetmeat glass on Silesian stem, *c*. 1725.

Mansell considered impossible. Lady Mansell was left in sole charge while her husband went off on an expedition to curb Mediterranean pirates. On the whole he was an unlovable man, as so many of his type, but he none the less conferred undoubted benefits upon the industry.

The Civil War put an end to the monopoly system, and it is thought that by about 1650 glass-makers scattered about the country were able to work as best they could without risking legal penalties. With the Restoration in 1660 (Mansell had died in 1656) George Villiers, the second Duke of Buckingham, became the most prominent person in the trade. He made mirrors at Vauxhall and table-glass at Greenwich, and, when practical glass-makers obtained a licence, instead of fighting them he employed them and turned their licence into a patent. Whether his various enterprises were, profitable however, is not known.

At this time important developments in the technical side of the industry took place in England, Germany and Bohemia. The two last-named countries devised a means of purifying their Venetian-inspired potash-glass by the admixture of lime; and England reached a similar result, after many experiments, by the use of lead-oxide, and so, for the first time, became both self-supporting and an exporter of glass. This consummation took several years, and was due, as most technical advances are due, to the ability of one man who happened to be backed by a band of shrewd traders who knew what the market required.

Evidence of the sort of thing which the English importer asked from Venice is provided by the records in the British Museum of a firm of glass-sellers, John Greene and Michael Measey, who had dealings with Allesio Morelli of Murano between 1667 and 1672. John Greene was a prominent member of the Glass Sellers' Company, and his papers show that he imported over one thousand looking-glass plates and two thousand dozen glasses; they also show that he complained continuously about quality and breakages, and in 1671 he gave a warning that he might be looking for future

63. Two members of the Kit-Cat Club by Kneller, *c.* 1710. They are Lord Lincoln and the Duke of New-castle.

supplies at home, by which one can deduce that English standards were improving. And indeed they were, for two years later George Ravenscroft (1618–81) set up his experimental glasshouse in the Savoy with the company's backing, employing Italian craftsmen as his assistants. The progress made was encouraging enough for the company to finance him further; he moved to Henley-on-Thames and continued his experiments. The result was at first imperfect glass-of-lead (for it was liable to 'crizzle'), but he was allowed to mark it with the seal of a raven's head. In 1678 he terminated his agreement with the Glass Sellers' Company; the reason is not known. He died three years later, so his retirement may have been due to ill-health and not to disagreement. His work was completed by Hawley Bishop, so that by the end of the 17th century the glass-of-lead formula had become standard and the days of Venetian dominance were ended.

It is perhaps curious that so little has survived from the days before the invention of this far superior material—that is from the time of Verzelini to that of Ravenscroft—which can definitely be accepted as of English manufacture. It is thought that Bowes and Mansell were content to produce the most ordinary expendable glass wares, with the result that what skill was available had little chance to embark upon finer work. The difficulty was brought home to us very effectively in the impressive exhibition organised at the Victoria and Albert Museum by the Circle of Glass Collectors in 1962, where out of eight glasses in the section labelled 'Anglo-Venetian' (17th century), the words Anglo-Venetian were put in inverted commas and only one of the eight was catalogued as English *tout court*, while the remaining seven were called 'Netherlandish, or perhaps English' or 'English, perhaps Venetian, but in soda-metal'.

Nor is everyone convinced that a famous goblet dated 1663 and diamond-engraved with portraits of Charles II, framed in oak branches, and of Catherine of Braganza, and inscribed 'Royal Oak', is entirely English (Fig. 55); it is in light greenish-brown metal in the Venetian manner and could have been made and engraved in any one of half-a-dozen glasshouses in the Netherlands. Similar doubts have been expressed about the English origin of a glass 17 in. high (a 'flute' glass), diamond-engraved with a bust portrait of Charles, a sprouting oak stump and the words 'God bless King Charles The Second' (Fig. 56). This was probably made for the King's Coronation, and the Royal Oak goblet commemorated his wedding. The usual comment on both these very interesting glasses is to suggest that they were made in an English glasshouse manned by Italians and engraved by a Flemish or Dutch workman.

64. Two English candle-sticks, *c.* 1730.

65. Three English candlesticks, *c.* 1730.

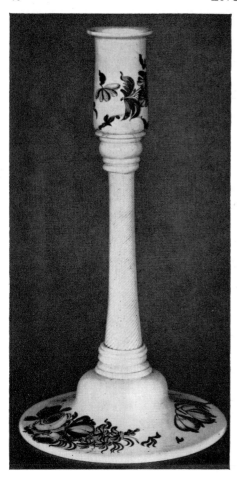

66. Opaque
English candlestick,
c. 1760.

67. English 'Amen'
glass.

In brief a definite English style did not make its appearance until towards the end of the 17th century. The industry must have been considerably indebted to the publication in 1662 of the standard Italian book on glass manufacture in an English translation by George Merret. This was *L'Arte Vetraria*, by Antonio Neri, published originally in 1612. Ravenscroft appears to have used ground flints instead of Venetian pebbles for his silica and at first added an excessive amount of alkali, which caused crizzling, or a network of cracks, in his first experimental glass. This fault was remedied by oxide of lead. The common and indiscriminate use of the terms 'flint glass' or 'glass-of-lead' is confusing: the product is the same, but the first emphasises the ground flints, the second the lead addition. It is curious to read that Neri was familiar with glass-of-lead—'as to colour the finest and noblest glass'—and lead was of course used in pottery glazes.

W. B. Honey, in his *Glass* (V. & A., p. 100), sums up as follows: 'The employment in glass mixtures of the oxide of lead called litharge was apparently new at this time and the use of this in combination with potash as the alkali was the special English contribution to glass-chemistry. At first added in small quantity the proportion was increased to as much as thirty per cent of the weight of the mixture. Though Neri had written in praise of the beauty of glass-of-lead, it is probable that lead was used by Ravenscroft at first merely to increase the fusibility of the mixture and it was formerly supposed that this increase was needed because the glass-pots had to be closed to keep out sulphurous fumes when coal fuel was substituted for wood; but this change took place at least fifty years before Ravenscroft's experiments. Something else made it necessary to increase fusibility, and this may have been the refractory English flint. Before long, however, sand replaced flint in English glass-of-lead, but the name 'flint glass' continued, and still continues, to be used for it.'

68. Three English wine-glasses.

Three illustrations have been chosen to represent Ravenscroft's immensely important contribution to this technological advance. The finest is perhaps Fig. 57 showing a jug nearly 11 in. high, with bold ribs, a spreading foot, also ribbed, and a massive rope-like handle. The decanter jug with a narrow neck, a wide mouth and a small collar seen in Fig. 59 is almost certainly by him. The bowl in Fig. 58—one of a pair of very remarkable objects picked up for next to nothing in a country sale near Tring in 1937—can be dated to 1676 by its engraving. One of them is diamond-engraved with the arms of Butler Buggin, of North Cray, Kent, the other with those of his wife, Winifred Burnett, of Leys, Aberdeen. The bowls are of lead glass and were presumably marriage gifts. The wedding took place in 1676, the year Ravenscroft began to work to his new formula. It was in the following year that his employers, the Glass Sellers' Company, authorised him to 'seal' his glasses with a raven's head as his signature.

The new metal met with immediate success. It was very different from all that had preceded it. It was very much heavier and so could not be blown out as thin as Venetian-type glass, but it possessed other notable virtues. It had a wonderful brilliance under every condition of light, whether natural or artificial, lent itself extremely well to all but the most exaggerated manipulations, and could survive more hazards than glasses made in the Venetian manner. Similar experiments designed to the same end, to break the near-monopoly of Venice, were being conducted at the same time in Germany and Bohemia, also with important results, though, in the opinion of most collectors, the metal produced (which included not lead, but potash instead of soda, and a high proportion of chalk) cannot compare with the soft dark brilliance of the English version. Bohemia seems to have been the first district to produce this metal, and its manufacture quickly spread over the whole of Germany.

69. English Williamite goblet.

In every country, design, whether in silver, furniture, pottery or other material, inevitably conforms to current fashions, and glass naturally followed the general trend of the late 17th and early 18th centuries—that is, away from the flamboyance which is one of the charms, if often an exasperating one, of the age of Charles II and his successor, towards a period when plain surface and finely balanced proportions were all that was required. The new metal can be said to have reached maturity by about 1700. The demand for ornament did not wholly die out, of course, and vessels which are ribbed or gadrooned (a favourite device of the silversmith), or 'wrythen' (that is, decorated with spiral or twisted reeding), or, in Ravenscroft's phrase, 'nipp'd diamond waies' (adorned with diamond-mesh in relief) continued to be made for several decades. But on the whole the most convincing triumphs of the glass made to the new standard are to be found among the simpler pieces, among which the covered goblet of Fig. 60 deserves a high place. This could scarcely be simpler: it appears to be from the last years of the 17th century.

From now on, we are confronted by an immense variety of glass designed for all kinds of domestic use—from wine-glasses to candlesticks, from bowls to chandeliers—and treated in every kind of technique—engraved, painted, cut or what have you. The commentary accompanying the illustrations now to be described endeavours to map out this wide territory in a logical manner without bewildering the reader with excess detail. There are numerous variants of the fine baluster stem of Fig. 60, which have been laboriously given labels, such as acorn, mushroom and angular knops. With the Hanoverian succession the fashion for a high-shouldered moulded stem, the so-called Silesian stem, became popular. It is a pleasant variation upon the baluster, and some consider that it was regarded as a compliment to the new dynasty, though George I had no connection with Silesia.

70. The Chastleton
House Jacobite glass.

71. Beilby landscape
glasses painted in
enamels.

Fig. 62 shows this stem used for a sweetmeat-glass, the upper part of which retains the 17th-century manner, but which presumably dates from the 1720s. The slender, graceful wine-glass of Fig. 61 probably dates from the same decade and is an obvious variant of the stem of Fig. 60. It is generally referred to as a 'Kit-Cat glass', after the famous painting by Kneller, now in the National Portrait Gallery, of members of the Kit-Cat Club (Fig. 63). The glass candlesticks of Figs. 64, 65 and 66, are singularly graceful examples—the first five dating from about 1730 and the sixth, opaque glass in imitation of porcelain and probably painted at Bristol by Michael Edkins, from about 1760. Whereas the baluster stem is necessarily made separately from the bowl, a stem which was first found in Venetian glasses and which remained in favour from the 17th century is the drawn stem, that is, one which is drawn out from the trumpet-shaped bowl in one piece. An exceptionally elegant specimen from the mid-18th century is seen in Fig. 67.

72. Series of typical English cordial glasses with Jacobite wine-glass.

The earlier drawn stem glasses often have a tear, or air bubble, in the stem, and from this the transition to a more elaborate means of decoration was logical enough. This is the air-twist, produced by drawing out and twisting the viscous glass containing one or more of these bubbles. The next step was to pick up one or more threads of opaque white or coloured glass into the lump of molten metal and manipulate the mass, as with the glass containing the air bubbles. It was a pretty novelty in high fashion in the 1750s and 60s. Sometimes air and opaque and coloured twists are combined in the same stem.

Wheel-engraving on glass, so popular in the Netherlands and in Germany, is rarely seen on English glasses. It is thought that a great deal of what has survived is the work of Dutch or German engravers living in England, with perhaps certain comparatively simple designs, such as the border of vine leaves in Fig. 68, as exceptions. Much English glass was exported, particularly from Newcastle, to be engraved in the Netherlands. In addition to these exceptions, there are the Jacobite glasses, which continue to exercise a compelling fascination, though it must be noted that, on the whole, their engraving cannot be placed in the top rank. A fine example of a Jacobite—in this case Old Pretender—goblet was seen at Sotheby's during the season of 1962–63. It is inscribed:

> Send him soon home
> To Holyruood House and that no Sooner
> than I do with Vive La Roy

—evidence more of enthusiasm than of good French. The same year saw the massive Williamite goblet of Fig. 69 in the same rooms. It is engraved with a portrait of William III and inscribed 'The Glorious and Immortal Memory of king William and his Queen Mary and Perpetual disappointment to the Pope the Pretender and all the enemies of the Protestant Religion'. A great deal, much of it excessively tedious, has been written about the significance of the emblems to be found on Jacobite glasses, which, in fact, continued to be made until the death of the Old Pretender in 1766; obviously the cause had long been lost and the Government of the day could afford to smile

73. Series of typical
English 18th-century
ale glasses.

74. Three late 18th-century or
early 19th-century English run-of-
the-mill jugs.

75. English decanter and two
tankards, engraved in Holland.

76. Three English bottles, early 19th century. The one on the right with portrait of Nelson.

at any sentimental toasts to the King Over the Water (one toasted him holding one's wine-glass over a glass of water). The chief emblem on these glasses, apart from the occasional portrait of Charles Edward, the Young Pretender, is the heraldic Rose with one or two buds; the Rose is held to represent the Crown, the bud the Old Pretender, the buds his two sons, Charles Edward and Henry. Many carry the inscription FIAT—'May it be so' i.e. 'May the King come into his own again'—or *Audentior Ibo*—'I will go forward more boldly'. In addition there have been recorded about twenty or so glasses engraved in diamond-point with a crown, the Cypher IR and RI entwined, as in Fig. 67, and with two or four verses of the Jacobite hymn on the bowl. This ends with the word

77. Early English bottles, 1770 and 1657.   78. Two English decanters, about 1780.

79. English cut glass of about 1810.

Amen and consequently such glasses are generally referred to as Amen glasses. Perhaps one verse is worth quoting:

> *God bliss the subjects all,*
> *And save both great and small*
> *in every station.*
> *That will bring home the King*
> *Who has the best right to reign,*
> *It is the only thing*
> *Can save the Nation.*

It is thought that the great majority of these glasses were engraved during the few years after the 1745 rising and that the spelling 'bliss' and the use of the Scottish title of James VIII point to a Scottish engraver. A decanter and six air-twist wine-glasses engraved with Jacobite emblems which had remained at Chastleton House, Oxfordshire, since they were made and which appeared at Sotheby's in the season 1961–62, are illustrated in Fig. 70. They were made for Henry Jones (d. 1761), who was an ardent Jacobite and a member of the Jacobite club at Gloucester.

By the Glass Excise Act of 1745 a duty was imposed upon glass by weight. This had two consequences; manufacturers endeavoured to find designs which would be lighter, and to attract purchasers by means of cutting or painted decoration. In the case of the latter method, mention has already been made of enamel painting on opaque white glass in imitation of porcelain (see Fig. 43, the chinoiserie vase, and Fig. 66, the flower-decorated candlestick). English painting in enamel on clear glass is confined to the remarkable brother and sister William and Mary Beilby, whose productions during their brief years of activity are among the finest of all glasses of the second half of the 18th century. Their work as glass enamellers seems to have been confined to the years between 1762 and 1778; they then went to Fifeshire. The most imposing of the Beilby glasses are some fine goblets painted with armorials, obviously special orders for particular persons. These were painted probably by William, for his sister was only thirteen in 1762. When a signature occurs it is Beilby without an initial, with one exception; there is a goblet in the Fitzwilliam Museum, Cambridge, painted with the

80. English Regency candelabra of ten lights.

Royal Arms and with the Prince of Wales's feathers and motto *Ich Dien* and signed W. Beilby. Apart from the heraldic painting there is a wide range of very charming rustic and fanciful subjects —peacocks, butterflies, ruins, etc.—mostly on smaller glasses. Fine examples of Beilby landscape and heraldic painting are illustrated in Fig. 71. A representative series of 18th-century glasses is illustrated in Figs. 72 and 73.

Cut-glass, which had been produced to some extent by the ancients, is supposed to have been first sold in England early in the 18th century by John Ackerman, who employed a German glass-cutter and in 1719 advertised that at the Rose and Crown, Cornhill, he continued to sell 'all sorts of tea, chinaware, plain and diamond-cut flint glasses'. 'Diamond-cut' means a pattern in the shape of diamonds. Revolving wheels are used to grind the surface, the edge of the wheels being flat, convex or V-shaped according to the type of cut required. The result, particularly in the case of the English glass-of-lead with its exceptional power of refraction, can be brilliant, and it is not surprising that cutting became more and more in favour, although the Excise Duty of 1745 had at first a limiting effect. This was because, with a duty of 1d. per lb. levied on weight, every manufacturer tried to make two glasses out of the metal formerly used for one; it followed that, as glasses became lighter, only shallow cutting was possible.

The trend towards lighter glasses became more pronounced with the increased excise duties imposed in 1777, 1781 and 1787. At the same time there was no excise duty in Ireland, and, after 1780, free trade obtained between the two countries. It brought a period of great expansion in the

81. English cameo portrait. Signature of the medallist Bertrand Andrieu.   82. English cameo portrait of Queen Victoria in a glass paperweight by Apsley Pellatt, *c.* 1840.

Irish glass industry, many workers and more than one employer going over from England. For instance, in the evidence given before the Committee appointed in 1785 to enquire into commercial relations between Great Britain and Ireland, it was stated that 'Mr Hill, a great manufacturer at Stourbridge, had lately gone to Waterford and taken the best set of workmen that he could get in the county of Worcester'.

From this and other statements many people have got the impression that there were no glass-houses in Ireland until the 1780s. In fact there was one of more than ordinary consequence, that established by Philip Roche in Dublin in 1690, and his advertisements listed the same goods as those in the English newspapers—all kinds of drinking-glasses, decanters, sweetmeat-glasses, candelabra, etc.

The best known of the later Irish glasshouses was that established at Waterford by George and William Penrose in 1783. In 1786 the two brothers petitioned the Irish Parliament in the following terms: 'Petition of George and William Penrose of Waterford stating that they had with great difficulty, and at the expense of nearly £10,000, established a complete flint glass manufactory. The works employ from fifty to seventy manufacturers who have mostly been brought from England at heavy expense. Since the factory was erected, the imports of flint glass into the kingdom had entirely ceased, and therefor ask for aid to carry on the manufacture.' The enterprise was carried on success-fully until 1851 and the term Waterford became synonymous with Irish glass in common speech.

There are still some people to be found who cling to the myth that Waterford glass can be dis-tinguished by a characteristic bluish tint to be found in no other product. The final word on the subject was written by Dudley Westropp, Curator of the National Museum, Dublin, in his *Irish Glass* (1920): 'I have never seen a marked Waterford piece with a blue tint.' Other glasshouses were established at about the same time at Belfast and Cork. Occasionally identification is made easy by a name impressed on the base of a vessel. The following have been recorded: Penrose, Waterford; Cork Glass Co., Waterford, Co. Cork; Francis Collins, Dublin; J. D. Ayckbown, Dublin; B. Edwards, Belfast; C. M. Co. (Charles Mulvaney, Dublin); Armstrong, Ormond Quay.

The style of all this Anglo-Irish glass from the 1780s to about 1825 has been described as classical-heavy; fashion demanded deep cutting wherever possible, combined with the slicing and fluting of the earlier, lighter types. The only marks, such as the names given above, appear on decanters and finger bowls, not, for some unexplained reason, on other productions. As happened with other crafts after the Napoleonic Wars, and in other countries, a new middle-class market and the increasing application of machinery to industry encouraged vastly increased production without the least improvement in public taste. But taste is a word loaded with emotion over which people can quarrel fiercely. Perhaps, though, it will cause little or no offence if I remark that designers in all Europe, and not only England, and in every field lost themselves in a jungle about 1830 and did not begin to emerge from it for another thirty or forty years.

The culmination of a vast amount of earnest enthusiasm was to be seen at the Great Exhibition of 1851 in the Crystal Palace—the first great building, by the way, to be made of glass. I quote Honey: 'Much stress was laid upon size, and there were exhibited monstrous cut-glass fountains and chandeliers, together with table-wares of cased glass cut and engraved in Bohemian style, and extravagantly blown and manipulated glass called "Anglo-Venetian", some of it frosted and gilded and of opal metal. Many bastard styles were named "Alhambra", "Grecian", "Egyptian" and the like and every resource in colour and in engraved and enamelled decoration was adopted with an exuberant and entirely uncritical belief in the value of applied ornament and mechanical ingenuity, and with a misguided enthusiasm for bizarre "artistic" forms.'

Figs. 81 and 82 are novelties from the Falcon Glasshouse in Southwark which belonged to Apsley Pellatt (1791–1863), who patented a process which he called 'Crystallo-cerami' or 'Cameo incrustation', and which, in his memoirs of 1821, he admits was communicated to him by 'a French gentleman'. The result was a lengthy series of portrait heads, figures and cupids, moulded in a porcellaneous material and embedded in glass: very pretty things, but not more than an extension in glass of the very similar cameo-reliefs of Josiah Wedgwood and James Tassie. The latter had made portraits and copies of engraved antique gems in a white paste from 1765. These Apsley Pellatt novelties are not to be confused with what, many years later, came to be called cameo glass.

By the middle of the 19th century wine bottles and decanters had been essential items in polite table-services for about one hundred and fifty years, sharing the honours of the table with the wine-bottles from which they derived. The early bottle form was a simple globe surmounted by a shaft; the earliest dated specimen of a sealed bottle in England is the one, dated 1657, preserved in the Central Museum, Northampton. The seal was an impressed medallion—owner's or merchant's mark, sometimes with place and date as well on shoulder or base. As the years passed, the body grew straighter until bottles as we know them today became more or less standardised. They were

83. Three English blue glass scent-bottles decorated in gilt.

84. Nailsea glass.

made in dark green glass, sturdy rather than elegant. As society became less rough it demanded something more sophisticated for the table, and the early decanter, in the new colourless glass, was the obvious answer. The early specimens which have survived resemble the bottles of their generation and have a projecting rim at the top for tying on the cork with string. Stoppers came in about 1750— at first the so-called 'spire' shape, then the 'disc', the 'mushroom' and, later still, the 'lapidary', i.e. a circular knob cut in facets over its whole surface. The barrel-shaped decanter came into fashion about 1775, and square decanters (known as 'squares') a little later. They were of cut-glass at first, afterwards of moulded glass, and few Victorian sideboards were without a set of three, generally in a wooden frame which could be locked (see Figs. 75 to 78).

In Fig. 83 are three pretty examples of late 18th-century workmanship—blue glass scent bottles decorated in gilt.

The name Nailsea is automatically given to any glass vessel with a striped or speckled appearance. There was in fact a notable glass-works at this place near Bristol between 1788 and 1873, but there is little doubt that the style, even if it originated there, soon spread throughout the country. The material is not fine flint glass, but coarse greenish bottle glass. It is suggested that it began with an attempt to avoid the excise tax, which, though it began in 1745 at 1d. per lb. by weight on flint glass, had become nearly $2\frac{1}{2}$d. by the time the Nailsea works started, whereas the duty on bottle glass was about $\frac{1}{2}$d. The flecks of colour would have been added to render simple domestic wares more attractive. More sophisticated decoration, it is thought, would have come later—that is, the numerous odds and ends of flasks, hats, walking-sticks and rolling-pins in coloured glass, and some attractive jugs, bottles and mugs decorated in bold white festoons (see Fig. 84).

Pressed glass was an American invention which had enormous commercial success and enabled glassware imitating the fashionable cut-glass of the day to be manufactured in vast quantities at small cost; it made an important contribution to the Great Exhibition and was largely responsible for changing an ancient art into a modern large-scale industry. It is generally assumed that the half century from, say, the accession of Victoria to 1887, was not marked by anything beyond technical accomplishments and lamentable imitations of the past. Again I quote Honey: 'The most remarkable (though also the most unfortunate) consequence of the Great Exhibition was a museum-taught revival of former styles of glassmaking . . . mechanical processes were frequently used where the models copied had been made and decorated by hand work only.'

85. English cameo glass by George Woodall.

Opinion today regards that judgment as over-harsh. It must be confessed, however, that it takes courage to wade through the vast output of those years and patience to dig out what seems to be of lasting value or what can lay any claim to originality. Imitations of the past, however ingenious, soon become boring. Cut-glass continued to be made with a tendency to more and more deep cutting and heaviness, and this was speedily imitated in pressed glass.

The beginning of a more logical approach to basic principles is to be seen in certain graceful wine-glasses and tumblers designed by the architect Philip Webb for William Morris as early as 1859 and made by the Whitefriars Glassworks in London (James Powell and Sons). A technically triumphant, but aesthetically insipid, achievement in so-called cameo glass aroused great interest at that time and has now (1966) attracted the attention of the international art market, with the extraordinary result that the red cameo glass plate of Fig. 85, made about 1890 by George Woodall, was bought for the Corning Museum in America for £7,600, a price far in excess of any sum previously given in the open market for a glass object, however rare. (This plate had appeared in a sale in the same rooms as recently as 1926 when it made £140.) Its origin goes back to the Portland Vase (Fig. 2), which had been a challenge to glass-makers ever since it was discovered and had defied all efforts at imitation. After the Great Exhibition of 1851, a Stourbridge glass-maker, Benjamin Richardson, offered a prize of £1,000 to anyone who could reproduce it. John Northwood (1836–1902), who had been one of Richardson's apprentices, succeeded in making a vase in cameo technique, known as the Elgin Vase because it was decorated with designs after the sculptures of the Parthenon. This was in 1873 after eight years' work, and he also succeeded in making a replica of the Portland Vase three years later. His son, John Northwood II, who died in 1960, was also highly skilled in this very tedious process. Among several other craftsmen George Woodall (d. 1925), who worked for Thomas Webb and Sons, Stourbridge, is the best known, and now that his pretty ladylike Venus and Cupid has attracted so much attention we shall no doubt hear a great deal more about him.

5. Chinese Glass

Considering the vast amount of research lavished upon Chinese painting, bronzes, jades and ceramics during the past half century, it is surprising at first sight that so little attention has been given to glass. The reason is that the Chinese themselves never seem to have paid much attention to it and, when they did, regarded it chiefly as a cheap and convenient substitute for jade and other hardstones. They certainly did not accord it the same standing as they gave to porcelain or jade, though a glass-house, together with workshops for other crafts, was established in the precincts of the Palace at Peking in 1680 by the Emperor K'ang Hsi. There are only a few scattered references to glass in Chinese writings and then mostly in connection with ceramics.

It is said that opaque glass of various colours, together with clear glass, was imported from the Western world during the Han Dynasty (206 B.C.–A.D. 220), but that the Chinese did not themselves manufacture glass until the 5th century A.D. On the other hand various glass objects specifically Chinese have been found in tombs in the neighbourhood of Loyang which could hardly have been made outside China—a fish-shaped girdle pendant, a cicada and a *pi* (a ritual object normally of jade). These were clearly placed in the tomb as a cheap substitute for jade. This site, we are told, might be as early as about 400 B.C. and is certainly not later than about 200 B.C. There were also some glass beads containing barium, a substance which is not found in Western or Near Eastern glass until the 19th century. All these objects were greenish or bluish and much decayed, and it has been suggested that they were made from imported glass melted down by the Chinese and reworked by them. The evidence, in short, is inconclusive.

Syrian glasses of the Roman period have been found in China, and many small objects, such as figures of animals, have been excavated in tombs of the T'ang Dynasty and later. Recently I was shown a remarkably fine head which seemed to be carved from glass and not from rock crystal and which from its style could be attributed to the Sung Dynasty. The whitish crizzled bowl of Fig. 86 with its spiral ribbing is an impressive example of what is believed to be late 17th-century production, and the smaller bowl and cover of Fig. 87, of about the same period and very similar to a shape

86. (*Below*) Ribbed Chinese bowl, late 17th century.

87. (*Right*) Chinese bowl and cover, diamond-engraved.

59

88. Chinese vase with mark of the Emperor Ch'ien Lung. 18th century, carved on the lapidary's wheel.

familiar in porcelain, is decorated with diamond-engraved cloud scrolls. Each is remarkable for the simplicity of its form and decoration. On the other hand the vase of Fig. 88, which bears the mark of the Emperor Ch'ien Lung (1736–95), is of blue and red glass and has been carved on the lapidary's wheel in a manner familiar enough with jades.

The vessels most commonly seen on the market are small snuff-bottles very cleverly made and coloured in imitation of various hardstones—onyx, chalcedony and so on—which were so much admired; they even imitate such unlikely materials as red lacquer and rhinoceros horn. Occasionally enamel colours are painted on clear or opaque-white glass, and, somewhere about the beginning of the 19th century, an unknown craftsman introduced painting on the interior instead of on the outside. It was a practice which required uncanny (some say misguided) skill and patience, and was more easily applied to crystal with its rougher surface than to glass. But little glass bottles treated in this manner have been painted down to our own day and are not by any means to be despised.

6. Germany and Bohemia

In spite of the very natural desire of the modern state of Czechoslovakia to disclaim any connection with its formidable neighbour on the other side of the mountains, it is next to impossible to write about the glass industry of one without reference to the other, because Silesia—using the same forests for fuel as Bohemia—became German during the 18th century, thanks to the strong-arm policy of Frederick the Great. Glass, of course, had been known and used throughout all this vast area since Roman times, a coarse, greenish, yellowish or brownish glass derived from potash instead of the characteristic Venetian soda-glass.

The distinctive German vessel for wine, the *Roemer*, made its appearance during the 15th century. In its elementary form it was a small cup or beaker decorated outside with spots or drops of glass; this developed into the form, familiar from the 17th century, seen in Figs. 102, 104, 105 and 106, that is with a stem impressed with a so-called raspberry pattern of raised dots, generally referred to, in England, as raspberry prunts. It was a thoroughly practical device, making the vessel more or less safe in the fingers, and, if one can judge by the number of times such glasses are seen in 17th-century Dutch paintings, they were probably manufactured in large numbers throughout the Netherlands, as well as in the Rhineland and throughout German lands. They continued to be made in the greenish 'forest-glass' (*Waldglas*) long after the Bohemian glass-makers had devised a method of decolourising the metal by the addition of lime.

Three characteristic German glasses are seen in Fig. 89—in the centre a *Roemer* of pale green glass supported on a massive hollow stem with four rows of raspberry prunts. This is 17th-century from the Rhineland. The two flanking it, that on the left 17th-century, engraved with an eagle, and the other late 16th-century, are first-class examples of the *Stangenglas*; the bands of stringing are

89. Typical German glass. A green glass *Roemer* and two examples of a *Stangenglas*.

61

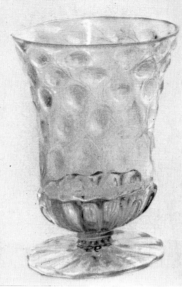

90. Three Bohemian beakers of about 1700. Beck Collection.

intended for measurement of the contents.

The ambition of all glass-makers was first to equal and then to improve upon the glass of Murano and so break the monopoly so long enjoyed by the Venetians. In England Ravenscroft's flint glass or glass-of-lead was produced. In Bohemia and Silesia a similar solution was reached by the invention of what, after much experiment during the 17th century, became known as Bohemian crystal— a hard, colourless, clear glass which, even if it did not possess the soft hidden fires of the English glass-of-lead, was endowed with great qualities and lent itself particularly well to engraving. By analogy with the much-prized rock crystal it was regarded as primarily a material for the lapidary. By the time this characteristic Bohemian metal was being produced in quantity, that is in the 1680s, there was an established tradition of engraving on glass. Its first practitioner, the jewel-cutter Kaspar Lehman, had been summoned to Prague by the Emperor Rudolf II and, as a reward for his work, had been given a title of nobility in 1609.

The wholly distinctive Bohemian style begins about 1680, with thick-walled goblets and covers, often fluted and decorated with engravings. These were of various kinds—views of towns, allegories of Peace and War, engravings of ships or traders' wagons or the occasional historical souvenir, such as a goblet with an equestrian portrait of Leopold I and the Sultan Mustapha II to commemorate a peace treaty with Turkey. Anger at the loss of Silesia to Prussia in 1742 is symbolised by a goblet engraved with the imperial two-headed eagle and allegorical figures of Bohemia and Silesia.

An unusual little beaker, almost certainly Bohemian, was seen in the Beck Collection at Sotheby's in November, 1964, gadrooned round the base and supported on a radially moulded foot and engraved with grapes growing from a single vine (Fig. 90B). Figs. 90A and 90C are beakers of about the year 1700 with a more typical type of engraving: the first wheel engraved with figures symbolising the continents, the other with figures of St Michael and of a queen in flowing robes. To many the finest of the pieces in this collection was the covered goblet of Fig. 91, carved in rock crystal style (the German term is *Hochschnitt*) in the form of a cornucopia. The bowl is deeply cut on either side with a bird of prey perched on foliage; the cover is surmounted by a stylised bud knop. This, with another of a slightly different type, both of about the year 1700, came from the glass-works owned by the Counts Schaffgotsch in the valley of Riesengebirge in Silesia and is a superb example of baroque exuberance. Its neighbour, made at Nuremberg in 1719 and important historically rather

91. Bohemian covered goblet *c.* 1700 from the
Schaffgotsch glass works, Silesia. Beck Collection.

92. German goblet engraved with portrait of
Prince Eugene and inscription by S. Schwartz,
Nuremberg. Beck Collection.

93. German ruby glass beaker, late 17th century.
Potsdam. Beck Collection.

than aesthetically, is by the engraver S. Schwartz and bears a portrait of Prince Eugene flanked by Mars and Bellona and a shield with an inscription (Fig. 92).

By the end of the 17th century Potsdam was producing a series of ruby glasses of high quality, of which the beaker of Fig. 93 is a worthy representative. It is carved in *Hochschnitt* with a Bacchanalian scene of amorini blowing trumpets, carrying swags of fruit and, on one side, leading a goat. The three pieces of Fig. 94 are Bohemian, the goblets of *c.* 1740, the covered beaker of *c.* 1791. The goblets are decorated in *Zwischengoldglas*, that is with engraved gold leaf between two layers of glass. They are splendid things of their kind, at once dignified and gay. The technique was devised about 1725 and used, naturally enough, for important commissions for pieces intended not for ordinary table use, but as presents. The themes were mostly hunting, coats of arms, legends from the lives of the saints, or hearty social occasions, as in these two goblets. That on the left of Fig. 94 shows a terrace on which two couples are conversing, a dolphin fountain and a gazebo being on the other side; on that on the right are a man presenting another to a girl, dogs, refreshments, servants and an inscription—'Long Live the Engaged Couple'.

With reasonable accuracy the beaker in the centre can be dated to about 1791 from its subject, the balloon ascent of Victor Lunardi over the harbour of Naples, king and bodyguard in the fore-ground. This continuous scene, carried out by means of coloured paper and straw between the two walls of glass, presents a light-hearted variety nearly unique of its kind. Enamel painting, mainly in black (*Schwarzlot*), was a distinguished method of decorating glass, the credit for which is given to Johann Schaper (1621–70), a painter of both glass and pottery working on his own account. He was

94. Two Bohemian goblets *c.* 1740, in *Zwischengoldglas* and a beaker and cover commemorating Lunardi's balloon ascent at Naples. *c.* 1791, Beck Collection.

95. Two enamelled German beakers and a *Humpen*. Left to right: 1697, 1638, and second half of 17th century. Beck Collection.

at Nuremberg in 1655 and at Ratisbon in 1644, and had numerous followers in both Germany and Bohemia. The beaker on the right of Fig. 95—also from the Beck Collection—depicting a boar at bay on a mountainous landscape, is of the late 17th century and, in his manner, painted in sepia. The other two glasses in Fig. 95 are Saxon and are painted in polychrome enamels. The taller is painted with two coats of arms and the date 1638 and the one on the left has the date 1697 and the arms of Augustus the Strong, King of Saxony and Poland. Such work was admired from the late 16th century onwards, in both Germany and Bohemia, not less than it is today, but it must be confessed that the painting is frequently coarse and uninspired and that the forms are clumsy.

A good example of late 17th-century Bohemian glass painting—a robust and endearing peasant style—is illustrated in Fig. 96, the square flask dated 1697 enamelled in colours with St Christopher carrying the Child Jesus. Next to it is a more sophisticated covered beaker from perhaps half a century later decorated in gilt with an anniversary ceremony.

The first half of the 19th century witnessed many technical advances, some of which were important, others merely conjuring tricks. Among those who made considerable contributions to the craft was the Viennese Anton Kothgasser (Fig. 97), originally a porcelain painter, who continued the tradition established by the two Mohns, father and son, of painting silhouettes and views. Finely decorated gift tumblers of the late 18th century and the first few years of the 19th were the work of an Austrian, J. J. Mildner—glasses with medallion panels and borders decorated on the inner side in gold-leaf and red lacquer let in flush with the surface in spaces exactly cut out to receive them.

96. Bohemian square flask enamelled with St Christopher, 1697, and gilt decorated covered beaker, 18th century. Beck Collection.

In post-Napoleonic times the public liked romantic views; it also liked colour, ruby red, greens, blues, amethyst, topaz, amber, greenish-yellow and yellowish-green. One Bohemian glass-works produced, about 1820, a dense black opaque glass known as *Hyalith*, another an almost opaque glass marbled in various strong colours patented under the name *Lithyalin* (Fig. 98). Engravers and cutters were numerous and accomplished, shapes ponderous, but not without liveliness. Many artists worked independently, some wandering as far afield as England and America, others meeting with success by working in the capital during the winter and following their clients to a fashionable watering-place during the summer. Such a personage was Dominik Bimann (1800–57), who worked mainly in Prague. Three characteristic engraved profile portraits by him, all of the 1830s, are illustrated in Fig. 100. The two roundels were designed to be mounted on ormolu stands. The beaker, engraved with the portrait of a young boy, has six horseshoe-shaped projections round the base.

Finally there is the tumbler in Fig. 101—date about 1840—an example of a technique much in favour during the mid-century—engraving a flashed or silver-stained surface to leave the subject

97. Two beakers by Anton Kothgasser. Vienna, *c.* 1820.

98. Bohemian jug of *Lithyalin* glass.

99. Three Bohemian pieces of the mid-19th century. Beck Collection.

100. Three Bohemian portrait glasses by Dominik Bimann, Prague, *c*. 1830. Beck Collection.

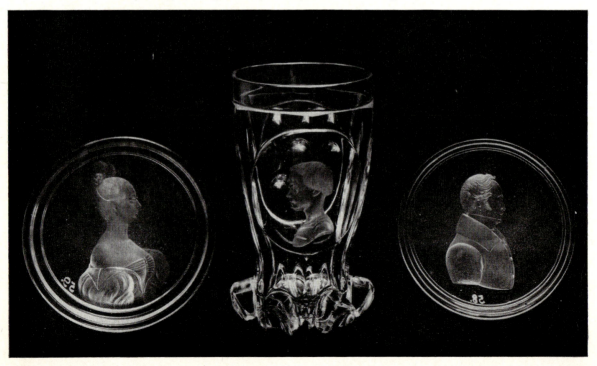

101. Bohemian
tumbler, *c*. 1840.

rendered in clear glass on a coloured ground, once again a form massive rather than graceful—and in Fig. 99 are mid-19th-century pieces which can perhaps be classed as entertaining oddities. The wine-glass is ruby-coloured, wheel-engraved with a stag-hunting vignette and a country house. The casket in the centre is ormolu-mounted, also of ruby glass, with a classical frieze for cover. Of the three the tumbler, with vertical panel cutting and gilded with a chinoiserie scene, is most comely: the sides are in marbled tones of amber, orange and grey. On the whole technical know-how, in Bohemia and elsewhere, was by this time in advance of taste.

7. The Netherlands

Workmen from Murano are recorded at Antwerp in 1541; by the end of the 16th century there were glasshouses at Liége, Huy, Maastricht, Middelburg and Amsterdam, and many more followed within the next hundred years. Inevitably, as elsewhere, the manner was predominantly Venetian, so that it is often a matter for argument whether a particular piece was made in Italy or by Italians or Italian-instructed workmen, in Amsterdam or Liége, or a dozen other places. While all generalisations are subject to exceptions, it is fair to assert that during the 17th and 18th centuries the glass of the Netherlands, and particularly that of Holland, was remarkable, not for originality of form or quality of metal, but for its decoration, which, whether diamond or wheel-engraved, reached an extremely high standard, partly professional, partly amateur. This decoration is of three kinds.

Up to about the end of the 17th century engraving with the diamond-point was a practice among cultured amateurs. Two 17th-century names are particularly well known. One is Anna Roemers Visscher, daughter of an Amsterdam merchant (1583–1651), who decorated German beakers and tall fluted goblets with flowers, fruit and insects. Occasionally she signed her work and the Rijksmuseum at Amsterdam possesses two dated glasses by her, one of 1621, the other of 1646.

On grounds of style the *Roemer* of Fig. 104 is sometimes ascribed to her; the engraving is of the greatest fluency and accomplishment. Her sister Maria (d. 1649) and a younger contemporary, Anna Maria van Schurman (1607–92), also worked in the same manner.

102. 17th-century still life by Floris van Schooten. A typical *Roemer*.   103. Dutch bottle engraved by Willem van Heemskerk of Leyden, 1674.

104. Netherlandish *Roemer* probably engraved by Anna Roemers Visscher *c.* 1650.

Anna Roemers was well known in her day as a woman of considerable learning and no mean poet. It is remarkable that at a time when the vast majority of women were tied to household duties and embroidery, engraving on glass should have been taken up by these few choice spirits. But there were, of course, other women in the Low Countries who were no less accomplished in other arts, notably the painters Judith Leyster and Rachel Ruysch. In Italy there was Artemisia Gentileschi. In England, as far as I know, no woman worked on glass until William Beilby's sister Mary helped her brother with his enamelling at Newcastle in the 1760s.

The second outstanding amateur of the period was the poet, dramatist and cloth merchant Willem van Heemskerk (1603–92), of Leyden, who added engraved decoration with his signature and date to

105. Netherlandish
Roemer engraved
with dancing
peasants, by Willem
Mooleyser, *c.* 1685.

106. Netherlandish diamond-engraved glass by G. V. Nes, *c*. 1687. Arms of William III and the United Provinces.

107. Netherlands. English glass, stipple-engraved by Frans Greenwood, 1728.

many glasses between 1648 and 1690. Fig. 103, a bottle with a flowing calligraphy, is signed by him and dated 1674 and bears a couplet in praise of wine, paraphrased from the Book of Ecclesiasticus. I leave the reader to judge—or to guess—whether the Royal Oak goblet (Fig. 55), with its portraits of Charles II and Catherine of Braganza, and the Exeter Flute, probably made for Charles II's coronation (Fig. 56), are Dutch or English. Expert opinion seems to be hopelessly divided on this point. The *Roemer* engraved with dancing peasants of Fig. 105 is by Willem Mooleyser, known from several diamond-engraved glasses dated between 1685 and 1697, while the larger *Roemer* of Fig. 106 is signed by an otherwise unknown man, G. V. Nes; it bears the arms of William of Orange and of the Seven United Provinces and is presumably of about the year 1687. Another large *Roemer*, also by Mooleyser, is dated 19th April, 1689 (i.e., eight days after the joint coronation of William and

108. Netherlands. English glass, engraved in stipple by D. Wolff. An anti-Orange Association, 1775–90.

Mary at Westminster). It bears the arms of the United Netherlands and of William III as King of Great Britain and Ireland. Both these *Roemers* are in the Victoria and Albert Museum.

The next fashion in glass decoration in the Netherlands was wheel-engraving. It was almost wholly German in manner and, it is thought, very largely the work of German craftsmen. The glasses used were frequently of English manufacture—a choice, as E. M. Elville and others point out, which was not surprising. The English lead metal, says Elville, 'was softer to the wheel and of a bright and lustrous quality that displayed engraved work to better advantage than the potash-lime glass of Bohemia which the Dutch artists had used as their earlier medium'. Betrothals, weddings, armorial and naval subjects were the chief favourites; the most accomplished of the Dutch wheel-engravers was Jacob Sang, who signed many glasses during the years 1752–62. Four bearing his signature are in the Buckley Collection at South Kensington. The following advertisement is from the *Amsterdam Courant* of 3rd April, 1753:

'Simon Jacob Sang, Saxon artist-glass engraver, resident in the Ondebrugsteeg at the corner of the Nieuwendyk in Amsterdam, makes it known that he cuts and engraves on English goblets, panes, cabinet-panels and box-lids the most fashionable curiosities known and practised in Holland, whether in large or small figures, in perspective or in relief, shallow or deepcut, on matt or rough grounds, polished figures, coats of arms, names in any type of script, emblems, half-lengths or other portraits, rock and scroll-work of the newest fashion, Ovidian and other stories.'

Concurrently with wheel-engraving the diamond point came back into fashion in a slightly different manner, in the form of stipple-engraving—that is, the method in which the diamond point was set in a handle, which was struck with infinite care with a hammer. The result is, of course, a series of dots on the darker ground of the polished glass rather as if the artist were working in white chalk on dark coloured paper. This is a method which can produce results of exceptional delicacy in accomplished hands. It is described by Honey graphically enough: 'the engraving seems to rest like a scarcely perceptible film breathed upon the glass'. The majority of the glasses decorated by Dutch and Flemish engravers in this manner are of English manufacture. The originator of this type of engraving upon glass was an amateur, Frans Greenwood (1680–1761), evidently of English extraction, but a native of Rotterdam, who from 1726 was employed by the municipality of Dordrecht. Numerous glasses by him have survived, the most famous of them a goblet in the Metropolitan Museum, New York, stippled all round with a figure symbolising the River Meuse in a garden with

109. Netherlands. English glass engraved in stipple by D. Wolff 1775–90, showing children and the word 'friendship'.

110. Netherlands. Engraved in the manner of Wolff by an unknown artist.

trees and fountain and dated 1728. Fig. 107 is a glass decorated by Greenwood of the same year—a man holding a *Roemer*. The fashion lasted until well into the middle of the 19th century; much of it is anonymous, most of it dextrous and charming, and Elville remarks that 'some specimens are of such evanescence as to be almost invisible in certain lights'.

The name of David Wolff (1732–98) used to be attached to the majority of the surviving examples from the last forty years of the 18th century, but it has long been realised that Wolff was only one among a great many competent engravers practising at the time. The term 'Wolff glasses' is still used to describe his style, represented here by three characteristic pieces, Figs. 108, 109 and 110. Fig. 108 commemorates an anti-Orange organisation and Fig. 109 is one of several charming glasses decorated with figures of children. Both are confidently attributed to Wolff. The armorial glass of Fig. 110 used to be thought to be by him, but is now recognised as being by a finer but anonymous hand. It is engraved with the arms of William and his consort, whom he married in 1677. Stipple-engraving has remained in favour in Holland down to our own day.

In the opinion of Dr Ferrand Hudig (*An Essay on Dutch Glass Engravers*, 1926), the last Dutch engraver of renown was the Amsterdam chemist D. Henriques de Castro, who died in 1863: 'He was a great amateur of engraved glasses and added many pieces by his own hand to his collection. He was experienced in all methods—engraving, stippling and etching—and not seldom we find all these methods applied in a single piece.' Hudig sums up in these words: 'Although with all its charm we cannot consider diamond-engraving an independent art, we must take it for what it was meant to be: delightful dilettantism.'

8. France

If this book were concerned with the history of mediaeval stained glass, or of mirrors, or of plate glass, at least half of it would be devoted to French artists and craftsmen. The chief centres were Normandy and Lorraine, but, though the manufacture of window-glass, whether clear or coloured and whether for French churches or for those of neighbouring countries, was an important industry for centuries, certainly from the 12th to the 16th century, for a very lengthy period the only vessels produced were simple wares made of the rough so-called greenish forest glass (*Waldglas* in German, *verre de fougère* in French). It is remarkable, perhaps inexplicable, that a country which contributed so much to the arts of civilisation should have, until recent years, taken so little interest for so long in so subtle and magical a material. The chief influence, as in other countries, was, of course, Italian, and no doubt there are numerous glasses in existence which could have been made just as easily by Italian workmen in Lorraine as by other Italians in Antwerp. The craft was held in high esteem and, from as early as the 14th century, was considered as one which could be practised by men of noble birth without loss of dignity or privilege. Garnier, in his *History of Glass*, 1886, summed up as follows: 'In France one remained noble although one was a glass-maker, at Venice one was noble

111. Three glasses in Venetian style, the one on the right possibly French, the other two Venetian. 16th or 17th century.

112. Nevers enamelled glass figures in papier-mâché pavilion, *c.* 1750.

113. French carafe and glasses made at Baccarat for Louis XVIII, *c.* 1818.

because one was a glass-maker and at Altare one was only a glass-maker because one was a noble-man.'

Occasionally a little light is thrown upon early obscurities, as when, in the 16th century, Ludovico Gonzaga married Henrietta of Cleves and so became Duke of Nevers. Italian glass-makers from Altare settled at Nevers and continued to make glass in Italian style until the 18th century, so that the town was described as 'Little Murano'. Their speciality, though, seems to have been small glass animals, and it is recorded that the boy Louis XIII, who was born in 1601, played as a child with these pretty toys from Nevers. He visited the town when he was twenty-one and was presented with an allegorical group in glass. More than a century later an array of glass figures on gilt pedestals was presented to the then duchess by the councillors. Though the fashion for these engaging novelties may well have originated at Nevers, it soon spread elsewhere, and by the 18th century glass toys were being manufactured not only in France, but also in Bohemia, Germany and England; a glass ship, for instance, in the Victoria and Albert Museum, its hull and rigging formed of glass threads, is reputed to have been made at Bristol.

As in the case of many other manufactures, Louis XIV's energetic minister, Colbert, took a hand in the encouragement of the glass industry, but the emphasis at this time—the second half of the 17th century—was on the making of mirrors (to break the monopoly of Venice) and on the exploita-tion of the important invention of the casting of plate glass, an invention due to the painstaking researches of a certain Bernard Perrot. Eventually, after various vicissitudes, the great works of St Gobain were established in 1693, and they have continued to produce plate and mirror-glass ever since. But so little progress had been made in producing table-glass that in 1760 the Académie des Sciences offered a prize for suggestions. The result was the foundation in 1765 of the famous factory at Baccarat, and two years later that of St Louis. Other smaller glasshouses were founded nearer Paris, and one was set up at Rouen by a Birmingham man, Mayer Oppenheim, with the published aim of making *cristaux blancs, façon et qualité d'Angleterre*. It is presumed that 18th-century glasses from these and other factories are so English in appearance that they cannot be identified.

114. French glass from the service made for the Elysée Palace.

A minor invention, usually credited to Apsley Pellatt in England, though, to do him justice, it must be recorded that he said in his memoirs that he learnt the technique from a Frenchman, was to enclose in white crystal glass white porcellaneous cameos and medallions. During the first part of the 19th century the French glasshouses followed in the main international fashions. A profitable and lively trade grew up in the 1840s, at both Baccarat and St Louis, in glass paperweights, now the darlings of the auction rooms and honoured by a regular bulletin, at least two learned, well-illustrated books and fabulous prices. This is a market rather like the vast stamp market, one in which values depend not upon aesthetics, but upon minute differences of pattern. But by 1820 the Baccarat standard was very high indeed, as witness the carafe and drinking-glasses of Fig. 113, made for Louis XVIII about 1818, and the glass from the modern service made for the Elysée of Fig. 114. As elsewhere the glass industry was due for a renaissance.

9. The Modern World

However technically advanced the first fifty or sixty years of the 19th century, however eager enterprising manufacturers to put novelties on the market, however adventurous their use of colour, in the main their products were run of the mill. Glass by now was no longer a luxury, but something without which a reasonably civilised existence was impossible. Its manifold uses for industry alone made it vastly important, and the more glass there was the more it was liable to be regarded as an industrial product rather than as a material suitable for an artist. One man, by his own endeavours and by the sheer force of his practical idealism, changed all that. The man was Emile Gallé (1846–1904), who, by 1865, was designing crystal ware for his father's table-glass factory at Nancy. Within fifteen years he was famous, the author of an enormous series of highly original vessels, at first of opaque, coloured, or marbled glass, then of transparent glass, decorated with enamelling, cutting, or engraving. Perhaps his most important, and certainly his most admired contributions to glass history were the numerous pieces he showed in the Paris Exhibition of 1889, evidently influenced by Japanese art—pieces in which he made use of flowers and leaves and foliage with extraordinary grace and sensitivity, as in the well known Oak Vase in the Victoria and Albert Museum (Fig. 115).

All this was something new, marked by a single, powerful and enthusiastic personality, with every technical process at his finger tips, and the designs were based upon nature. It was not for nothing that he was also devoted to gardening. His influence was enormous and, though modern criticism sees that, towards the close of his successful and honoured career (at one time his factory employed

115. French Oak Vase by Emile Gallé, 1889.

116. Two characteristic vases by Tiffany, New York.

three hundred people), there was some falling off in the quality of his work, he remains the one great pioneer of the last hundred years. Until his day a signature on a glass was as rare a phenomenon as water in the Sahara; Gallé signed his work and in so doing helped the public to realise that so marvellous a material, handled by a man of talent, could be a great deal more than a useful industrial product. His ideas were taken up with enthusiasm both in his own country and elsewhere. The nearest to him in spirit were the two brothers Daum, Auguste and Antonin, in Nancy, who also made glass decorated with flowers and leaves, and similar experiments were carried out at Sèvres and at Lunéville, in Belgium at Val-Saint-Lambert, in Sweden at Kosta and elsewhere and also in Norway. This was factory work, but at the same time a few independent studio artists were also making their small, but not unimportant, contribution to the craft—people like Brocard, who specialised in enamel glass, and a certain A. Jean, primarily a potter. Mrs. Ada Polak makes the shrewd comment: 'Perhaps it was the fact that the young French art of glass was grafted on to the nation's solid old ceramic tradition that gave it its astounding technical quality and surprising air of sophistication right from the first.' Half-way between porcelain and glass was the material known as *pâte de verre*, a composition of powdered glass which could be coloured and moulded; several people, and occasionally Gallé himself, worked in this slightly translucent substance.

Though Gallé was the outstanding personality among artists in glass in Europe during the last twenty years of the 19th century, L. C. Tiffany (1848–1933) comes very close to him. Tiffany's father was a New York dealer in jewellery, antiques and modern applied art. The firm had branches in Paris and London and the young Tiffany had ample opportunities for study and travel. He became

117. Part of a service designed by Philip Webb for William Morris in 1859 and executed by James Powell and Sons.

specially interested first in stained glass for windows and then in blown glass. He was in Europe in 1889, and it is thought that his new thinking about glass must have been stimulated by Gallé's display at the World Exhibition in Paris in that year. By 1892 his firm was reorganised as the Tiffany Glass and Decorating Company, and in 1893, at the Tiffany Furnaces, Corona, Long Island, he began operations, assisted by a team of expert glass-blowers. He was an immediate success, in both America and Europe, and his work and that of Gallé are now studied with closer attention than previously because the distinctive style that both men, perhaps unconsciously, adopted, that is, *Art Nouveau*, with its flowing curves, is once again in favour. Some of his shapes suggest flowers or trees, and all are made in a great variety of shades. He found a method of giving his glass the metallic iridescence which he himself says he admired in excavated Roman glass. In his firm's booklet of 1896 this iridescence is said to have been achieved 'by a careful study of the natural decay of glass and by checking this process, by reversing the action in such a way as to arrive at this effect without disintegration'. The booklet describes 'how sections like of pearl or of onion appear on the surface, and how, when two of these meet, like the rings round two knots of wood, the curves of decomposition unite and form sinuous lines'. To achieve this was the ambition of every worthwhile artist of the 1890s.

It is possible that this great American will be best remembered for his glass. This he would have wished, but it is relevant to note that his influence was important in other directions as well—in the worlds of ceramics, of jewellery and of metalwork, and in interior decoration generally (Fig. 116).

No fashion lasts for ever. In the glass world *Art Nouveau* had a longish run—from about 1890 until the time of the first World War. After that glass designers followed the fashion set by architects, with their insistence upon stark simplicity. Ornament was used sparingly, shapes were disciplined, style was formal. The great individual artist in glass between the wars was Maurice Marinot (1882–1960), friend of Derain and Segonzac. He began as a painter and first interested himself in

118. Stipple-engraved glass by Laurence Whistler.

glass in 1911, designing the forms and then decorating with enamels. He experimented at the furnace itself and from about 1922 until 1937 blew all his glass personally, working with inlays of colours between layers of transparent glass or with clouds of air-bubbles. All his glass is now in public or private collections and Mrs Polak was not able to trace a single piece in England. He was a fortunate man, untroubled by money matters and able to express himself as he wished. Like his predecessors he exerted immense influence among both studio artists and commercial enterprises.

The second great name between the wars and, probably because of its owner's immense factory output, better known than that of Marinot, is René Lalique (1860–1945). He became famous at the Paris Exhibition of 1900 as a designer of jewellery. He is best known not for blown glass, which he made before the first World War, but for the great array of vases and bowls, mostly of coloured glass with a frosted surface made after 1908 at his factory at Wingen-sur-Moder, on the German frontier. Animals, flowers, fish, women, are his main decorative motifs, but he produced well-disciplined formal designs far removed from the easy naturalism of the Gallé style. Most of his pieces were turned out by the press by the dozen, though occasionally he devised glasses of a more monumental type which had to be made singly.

Meanwhile the great Baccarat factory, while remaining faithful to its century-old tradition of cut-glass, began the production of a long series of clear pieces of exceptional purity of material and suavity of form, venturing occasionally into glass sculpture, as in the highly impressive *Le Coq*

Gaulois of 1954. The Daum firm experimented with shapes which can be compared with those of sculptors of the calibre of Barbara Hepworth.

Britain, with a firmly established public demand for its traditional cut- and engraved glass, has been slower to experiment. That ideas were still possible of occasional fulfilment during an unlikely period is shown to perfection by the three glasses of Fig. 117, which anyone could be forgiven for dating within the past thirty or forty years. They are in fact part of a set designed by the architect Philip Webb for William Morris in 1859—and executed by James Powell and Sons—superb objects, comely and practical and far in advance of their time. Not many people will disagree with the opinion that we have not since greatly improved upon Philip Webb's design for a table-service.

Decorative pieces—the more usual, but odious, term for them is 'art glass'—naturally followed

119. Zodiac dish by Steuben, design by S. Waugh.

120. Swedish glass engraved by Edward Hald, *c.* 1923.

current fashions, including a decidedly mild version in the 1890s of *Art Nouveau*; and, as elsewhere, something which could without much exaggeration be labelled a renaissance began in the 1920s and has not yet worked its way out. The trend has been towards simplicity, with occasional excursions into colour and a good deal of distinguished engraving in which the Whitefriars firm and the factories in the Stourbridge area (so long an important centre) and at Edinburgh have all played their part, with encouragement from the Royal College of Art and the Edinburgh College of Art.

Among the work of independent engravers that of Laurence Whistler is probably the best known today—a highly individual style, mainly executed in stipple (Fig. 118). He began by scratching lines of poetry on windows to amuse himself and his friends, and he later decorated wine-glasses, sometimes fine early examples, in diamond-engraving for individual patrons. A new impetus has been given to the craft in recent years by the engraving on the doors of Coventry Cathedral by John Hutton. This is breath-taking work on the largest possible scale. A technique once considered suitable only for small domestic objects is now seen as being capable of making an impressive contribution to the grandest architectural conceptions no less than stained glass itself.

The Steuben factory in the state of New York was founded in 1903 by a Stourbridge glass-maker

121. Swedish 'Graal glass' by Simon Gate, 1918.   122. Swedish glass by Edward Hald, 1930.

to make decorative glass. In 1918 it was absorbed into the vast industrial enterprise of the Corning Glass Works, whose museum now dominates the market for early glass. By the 1930s a new crystal glass had been evolved and the moving spirit of the plant was the great-grandson of the founder of the Corning plant, A. A. Houghton, Jun., who reorganised his inheritance on modern lines and so made at least as important a contribution to glass development in the United States as Tiffany had before him. His theory that if one man was responsible for both design and production the result was likely to be a mere technical exercise is open to argument—one presumes that Gallé thought otherwise—but there is no gainsaying the success of Steuben, or the quality of its productions, or its enterprise in employing outside painters and sculptors from all over the world to supplement the work and fertilise the ideas of its designers (Fig. 119).

If France and America set the pace during the final years of the 19th century, Scandinavia, and especially Sweden, has led the field during the 20th, thanks partly to an inherited tradition of well-balanced simplicity in all the applied arts—furniture and textile design developed on parallel lines—and partly to the foundation of the Swedish Society of Industrial Design as early as 1845, but mainly to the employment by industry of unusually gifted men and women. As elsewhere, a Venetian was working in a Swedish glasshouse as early as 1571, but Swedish glass of the 17th, 18th and 19th centuries is very largely copied from current German productions.

During the first World War a wholly original chapter in glass history began to be written at Orrefors in Southern Sweden, when two men of outstanding ability, Simon Gate and Edward Hald, both trained as painters, were appointed as designers (Figs. 120–123). A certain degree of war

123. Three Swedish glasses by Simon Gate, 1932.

austerity doubtless had something to do with the theories then in vogue about fitness for purpose—
functionalism as it came to be called—but nowhere else in Europe were these theories interpreted
with more imagination. The first glass designed by these two pioneers was a service of table-glass,
and then came a succession of more ambitious decorative forms and the production of the so-called
Graal glass (very close to Gallé's manner), which became a starting-point for a much admired
service of glasses in colour. The best known of the Orrefors productions outside Sweden has been
the engraved glass, by both Gate and Hald, which achieved immense success during the 1920s—
elegant, sturdy, neo-classical designs, often witty and gay, and the perfect complement to the
architecture of the time, of which the town hall of Stockholm is so admirable an example. Later
Graal glass developed on massive lines with the ornament embedded in the casings and was combined
with what was described by the factory as 'organised air-bubbles'.

The Orrefors success encouraged many other factories both in Sweden and elsewhere in
Scandinavia. It still remains the centre of the country's glass industry and shows no signs of failing
vitality. Kosta is an enterprising rival, and, in addition to these two, there are more than a dozen
factories in Sweden which work under the direction of professional designers. The trend now is
away from the more complicated models towards a plainer manner, often in tinted glass. A third
great name, apart from Gate and Hald, is that of Edward Strömberg (who died in 1946), ably
assisted by his wife Gerda (d. 1960). 'Strömberg,' remarks Mrs Polak, 'never made coloured glass—
it was the limpid transparency of crystal that fascinated him. The metal he made was pleasantly
firm, though soft in consistency, and gently toned towards grey, mauve or a very pale blue, and its

124. Bowl by Keith Murray, executed by James Powell and Sons *c*. 1935.

125. Czechoslovak vase and bowl, 20th century.

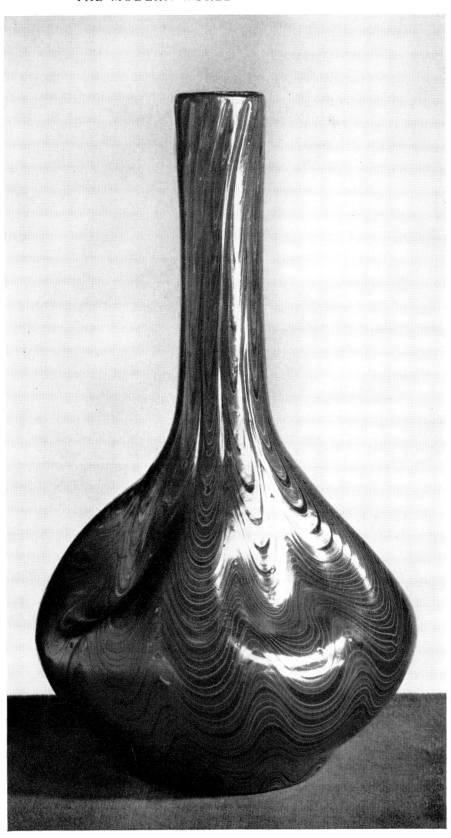

126. Czechoslovak
vase, 20th century,
from Lötz Witwe.

127. Glass, perhaps
Czechoslovak. Diamond-
engraved in England
by Mrs P. M. Boissier.

beauties were brought out in all their subtleties in the pure and sober forms designed by his wife, where the curve of a line or the gently increasing or decreasing thickness of material can suddenly reveal the finest shades of texture and tone.'

Denmark, Finland, Norway and Western Germany have followed a similar path, while Venice has continued to exploit age-long traditions of colour and manipulation (Figs. 128 and 129).

In spite of two devastating wars the 20th century has been a time of extraordinary achievement in the use of colour and engraving, and in the quality of the metal itself. At about the time of the first World War the industry began to employ designers trained in other fields. Gate and Hald, for instance, were painters (the latter, as one could guess from some of his engraved glasses, studied under Matisse); the Dane, Jacob Bang and the Englishman, Keith Murray (Fig. 124) were architects. Today designing for industry is a profession, and it may be that the danger for the future in all countries is that the designer may lack the *feel* of the material, which can be acquired only by actual work at the furnace. On the other hand too great an application to the merely manual part of the operation can stultify the imagination and make a man a skilful manipulator hidebound by routine. Somewhere a balance has to be struck. Commerce is a hard taskmaster and not every glass-works can flout public taste, which, except in very exceptional circumstances, is rarely anything but conservative. Miracles have been accomplished in the glass world during the last half century— an exciting half century, so stimulating in this (and in other) fields that one regrets that it is not yet normal to live to be a centenarian.

THE MODERN WORLD wait

128. Clear glass. Powdered gold inside, streaked decoration outside under an outer casing of clear glass by Ercole Barovier, Murano, 1951.

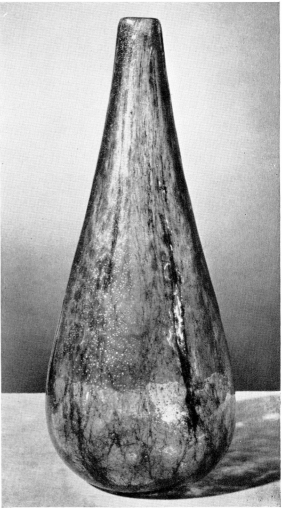

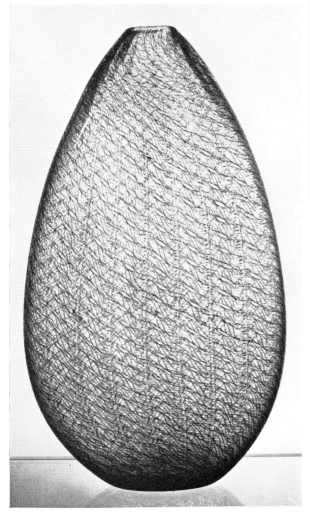

129. Clear glass with threaded decoration by Seguso Archimede, Murano.

Bibliography

Among many books and articles on glass, the following modest selection is recommended.

A. Hartshorne   *Old English Glasses*, 1897, London

W. B. Honey   *Glass*. A Handbook and a Guide to the Museum Collection. Victoria and Albert Museum

Frederic Neuberg   *Glass in Antiquity*. Translated by R. J. Charleston, 1949, Art Trade Press

Ferrand Hudig   *Dutch Glass Engravers*, 1926, Privately printed

Wilfred Buckley   *The Art of Glass*, 1939, Phaidon Press

Giovanni Mariacher   *Italian Blown Glass*, 1961, Thames and Hudson

E. Barrington Haynes   *Glass Through the Ages*, 1948, Penguin Books

E. M. Elville   *The Collector's Dictionary of Glass*, 1961, Country Life

E. M. Elville   *English Table Glass*, 1951, Country Life

E. M. Elville   *English and Irish Cut Glass*, 1953, Country Life

Alice Frothingham   *Spanish Glass*, 1964, Faber and Faber

Hugh Wakefield   *Nineteenth Century British Glass*, 1961, Faber and Faber

Ada Polak   *Modern Glass*, 1962, Faber and Faber

Derek C. Davis   *English and Irish Antique Glass*, 1964, Arthur Barker

Geoffrey Wills   *The Country Life Pocket Book of Glass*, 1966, Country Life

Index